Meeting Up with Grief Face To Face

How to Cope with Grief at Your Own Pace and Honor the Love That Remains - Even If You Feel Broken, Alone, or Overwhelmed by Guilt, Anger, Fear, or Resentment

Nicole De Coteau

© **Copyright 2025 - All rights reserved.**

The content contained within this book may not be reproduced, duplicated or transmitted without direct written permission from the author or the publisher.

Under no circumstances will any blame or legal responsibility be held against the publisher, or author, for any damages, reparation, or monetary loss due to the information contained within this book, either directly or indirectly.

Legal Notice:

This book is copyright protected. It is only for personal use. You cannot amend, distribute, sell, use, quote or paraphrase any part, or the content within this book, without the consent of the author or publisher.

Disclaimer Notice:

Please note the information contained within this document is for educational and entertainment purposes only. All effort has been executed to present accurate, up to date, reliable, complete information. No warranties of any kind are declared or implied. Readers acknowledge that the author is not engaged in the rendering of legal, financial, medical or professional advice. The content within this book has been derived from various sources. Please consult a licensed professional before attempting any techniques outlined in this book.

By reading this document, the reader agrees that under no circumstances is the author responsible for any losses, direct or indirect, that are incurred as a result of the use of the information contained within this document, including, but not limited to, errors, omissions, or inaccuracies.

Contents

Introduction	5
1. Meeting Grief at the Door	9
2. Shock, Numbness, and the First Waves	26
3. Facing Life Without Them	39
4. Anger, Resentment, and the Why	50
5. Guilt and Bargaining	63
6. After the Storm-Tools for Gentle Healing	77
7. Weathering the Middle—Living With the Absence	92
8. The Long Grief-Making Meaning Beyond the Years	106
9. Grief That Lingers, and What to Do About It	118
Conclusion	135
Dear Heart	139
Thank You Note	141
References	143

Introduction

You will lose someone you can't live without, and your heart will be badly broken... But the person lives forever in your broken heart that doesn't seal back up. And you come through. It's like having a broken leg that never heals perfectly—that still hurts when the weather gets cold, but you learn to dance with the limp.

— Anne Lamott

Grief changes you. And it does so without asking. It doesn't arrive gently, doesn't knock softly at the door. It crashes in—loud, uninvited, unapologetic—and nothing is ever the same again. It tears through the center of your life, rearranging everything: your priorities, your sense of time, even your sense of self. When the dust finally settles, you look around and realize you're not just grieving the person you lost—you're also grieving the version of *you* that existed when they were still here.

This book is about learning how to live in the after. In that strange, echoing world where nothing feels quite real and everything demands more energy than it used to. It's about what happens when you're handed a life you didn't choose—a life that includes loss as a permanent companion—and asked to find a way to keep going anyway.

We're told from an early age that time heals all wounds. It's meant to comfort us, this idea that we just need to wait long enough for the pain to fade. But the truth is, time doesn't heal in the way we're promised. Time is not a healer so much as it is a witness. It does not erase your grief—it simply gives you space to learn how to carry it. Not with less pain, necessarily, but with more grace. You grow stronger not because the weight has lessened, but because your muscles for holding it have. You don't stop missing them, you just learn how to live with the missing.

That's what Anne Lamott's quote gets so right. It doesn't pretend grief has a clean resolution or a polished moral. It tells the truth: That some losses break us in ways we never fully recover from. That the heart doesn't seal back up. That we're changed—permanently. But it also offers something softer, something profoundly human. You *do* come through. Maybe with a limp. Maybe with a heart that aches on certain days, like an old wound that remembers the cold. But you learn to live again. To move again. To dance, even differently, yes, but beautifully still.

When my mother passed away, my entire world shifted. Grief came in waves, which I was unprepared for—some gentle, some crashing. There were days I couldn't find the words to express what I felt inside, and other days when all I had were tears. Writing became my lifeline, a way to honor her memory and make sense of the pain.

This book isn't a blueprint for healing, and it's not a tidy self-help manual. It won't give you seven steps to closure or teach you how to rise from the ashes with glitter in your hair. Because real grief doesn't work like that. It's not a process you complete or a puzzle you solve. It's a landscape you learn to inhabit—a strange, emotional geography that shifts under your feet, sometimes daily. One moment you feel like you're doing okay, and the next, a scent or a song pulls the air from your lungs. You're not failing. You're just grieving.

So here, we won't try to outpace the sorrow or silence it. We'll sit with it. We'll name it. We'll learn to recognize its many forms—numbness, rage, exhaustion, longing—and treat them not as problems to fix, but as signs that your heart is still trying. Grief, after all, is not a disorder. It is not a weakness. It is not a sign that something has gone wrong. It is a sign of love that still lives, even when the person is gone.

Whether your grief is fresh or long-standing, loud or quiet, clean or complicated, you are welcome here. You don't need to be at any particular "stage." You don't need to be wise, or strong, or even functional. All you need to be is honest with yourself, with your pain, with your love. That's what this space is for. Not to fix the unfixable, but to be with you inside it. To make room for the truth of what it means to survive something you never thought you could.

You will grieve forever. But forever isn't only sorrow. It's also memory. It's also the shape of love after death. It's the way your voice softens when you speak their name. It's the way you carry them into every new chapter, not because you haven't let go, but because they are part of your story now, and always.

So, let's begin. Not with answers, but with presence. With honesty. With open hands and tender feet. Let's begin exactly where you are—in the wreckage, in the fog, in the in-between.

Let's begin.

Chapter 1

Meeting Grief at the Door

The risk of love is loss and the price of loss is grief. But the pain of grief is only a shadow when compared with the pain of never risking love.

— Hilary Stanton Zunin

When my mother died, the world didn't pause. People still went to work, answered emails, and bought groceries. But for me, time had split in two: *before* and *after*. The days surrounding her death—especially just before my birthday—now feel like sacred ground. Not a wound, but a place I return to each year with trembling hands and a full heart.

I used to think grief was something I had to "get through." Like a tunnel, or a mountain I was supposed to climb. But it's not. It's something I carry. And the weight shifts—some days it's a whisper, other days it knocks the wind out of me.

There are moments I still reach for the phone, forgetting she's gone. Or I hear her voice in a dream and wake up crying.

Grief doesn't ask us to forget. It doesn't ask us to "move on." It asks us to love differently. To find new ways of holding what is no longer here.

This chapter is not a blueprint. There is no one right way to grieve. What I offer instead is an invitation: To be tender with yourself. To let your grief be what it is—ugly, beautiful, loud, silent, raw, confusing. And to know you're not alone.

Grief will change you. But maybe—just maybe—it can also deepen you. Open you. Soften you toward yourself.

Let's begin there.

The Many Faces of Grief

Grief is the air you breathe after a loss; the weight that sits on your chest; the absence that hums in the background of every moment. It doesn't arrive all at once, and it doesn't leave in a straight line. It shifts, it transforms, it doubles back. Some days, it's a whisper. Other days, it's a roar.

And it doesn't look the same for everyone.

When You Lose a Spouse

The death of a partner—whether from illness, accident, or slow separation—is more than just the loss of a person. It's the loss of a shared *life*. It's waking up to an empty side of the bed and wondering who you are without the person who used to say "good morning" and "goodnight." It's opening the closet and seeing their clothes still hanging there, as if they could still somehow walk back through the door.

Everything changes. Your routines, your rituals, the rhythm of your days. Even the way you laugh changes, because they're not there to hear it. You feel like half of you has gone missing.

The feeling of disorientation. A haunting echo of what was. And yet, even in that void, love doesn't stop. It lingers in the everyday moments, asking to be carried forward in a different way.

When You Lose a Child

There are no words big enough for this. The death of a child is grief in its rawest, most feral form—whether it's from a miscarriage, a stillbirth, or a child who lived and laughed and then was taken.

It's a love with no outlet. It's the future you imagined, pulled out from under you. It's the toys that don't get played with. The birthday that comes without candles. The name you keep saying just to hear it.

Some days, it feels like you're the only one who remembers. But if you're reading this and nodding, know this: You remember because they mattered. And they still do.

When You Lose a Parent

This grief does not obey the logic of age. It doesn't matter whether you're 25 or 65. When a parent dies, something foundational shifts. You might be grown, independent, perhaps even a parent yourself, but deep down, an inner child still looks for them. Still hopes they might call. Still believes that somehow, their voice will be the one to make things okay again.

It doesn't matter what your relationship looked like from the outside. Maybe you were close, tangled in each other's lives in a way only parents and children can be. Maybe it was complicated—strained by distance, misunderstanding, or years of silence. Or maybe it was ambiguous, marked by hurt that never quite had the time or language to heal.

But even in the messiest relationships, there is often a quiet, stubborn hope. A hope that one day, things might shift. That one day, they'd finally understand you, that they might say sorry, or that you might find the words to forgive. When they die, that hope dies too. You grieve not just the person, but the possibility of what could have been.

When You Lose a Grandparent

Grandparents are often the storytellers, the keepers of family traditions, and their love is often a gentle, uncomplicated, and forgiving kind.

When they're gone, you miss their presence as well as what they represented: continuity, history, legacy. The thread that tied the past to the present. The person who always had hard candy in their pocket or a nickname for you that no one else used.

A friend of mine once described losing her grandmother *"like someone turned off the porch light and closed the door."*

It was simple, but it said everything. That feeling of warmth and welcome is suddenly gone by losing the one person who always made you feel like you belonged, no matter what.

When You Lose a Friend

Friends are the family we choose. They're our mirrors, our co-conspirators, the ones who remind us who we are when we forget. When you have friends, real friends, you have someone who sees the unedited version of you and stays.

Losing a friend, whether through death, distance, or the quiet drift that sometimes happens between people, can feel like losing a part of your own story. Their absence echoes in the casual places—your phone, your routines, your inside jokes, the parts of yourself you didn't share with anyone else.

It's a grief that doesn't always come with casseroles or sympathy cards. There's no formal mourning for friendship lost, even though the ache can run just as deep. But it deserves reverence. Because when a friend is gone, the world feels a little less like home.

When You Lose a Pet

They say it's *just* a pet, but anyone who's truly loved one knows it's never just that.

I was just a little girl when I came home from school one day, expecting the usual joy: My puppy racing to the door, tail wagging wildly, eyes full of love. But instead, I was met with silence and news that shattered my world. A tragic accident had taken my best friend, and in that moment, something in me broke.

The grief was real, raw, and far too big for words, far too heavy for a child to carry.

If you've ever known the love of a pet, you understand. They aren't "just animals." They're your safe place, your comfort, your partner in mischief and stillness. Whether it was the playful bark, the soft purr, or the gentle nudge when you needed it most, they brought a kind of magic—a steady, unconditional love that wrapped itself around your heart.

When they're gone, the world feels offbeat. Quiet. Empty. You wait for the sound of their paws, the warmth of their welcome, the routine that's now just a memory. And the silence, it hurts in ways only love can.

But even in that silence, they're still with you. In the rustle of leaves on your favorite walk, in the sunny spot where they used to nap, and in every instinctive glance at where they should be.

Because love like that leaves a mark—not just in photographs or memories, but in something deeper.

A paw print, forever etched on your heart.

The Losses That Are Harder to Name

Some griefs don't come with funerals. Some don't come with closure. There's the grief of estrangement, when someone is still alive but no longer in your life. The grief of dementia, where you lose someone slowly, piece by piece. The grief of addiction, of watching someone disappear into a version of themselves you no longer recognize.

And then there's disenfranchised grief—the kind the world doesn't acknowledge. The loss of a pregnancy, people tell you to "move on" from. The death of an ex you're not "supposed" to mourn. The heartbreak of a relationship that ended without death, but with just as much sorrow.

These griefs are lonely. They often come without support or ceremony. But that doesn't make them any less real. They still shape us.

Let Every Grief Be Welcome

Every loss touches the heart in its own way. Some arrive like fire—sudden, searing, impossible to ignore. Others settle like ice —slow, quiet, and numbing in ways you don't even notice until something finally cracks. Some knock you flat without warning.

Others wear you down grain by grain, until one day you realize you're not standing as tall as you used to.

But every single one matters.

Yet, in a world that moves fast and asks us to move with it, there's often an unspoken pressure to hold it all together. To be strong. To stay productive. To keep smiling, so no one gets uncomfortable. Grief doesn't always get permission to show itself, especially when the loss isn't seen as "big enough" or "public enough."

So, we tuck it away. We carry it on our shoulders, our stomachs, and our sleep. We show up, day after day, while part of us quietly falls apart behind the scenes.

But here's the truth: Whatever shape your grief has taken, whatever form your loss arrived in—death, distance, disappointment, dreams deferred—you have the right to feel it. To fall apart. To not be okay.

You are a human being, not a machine. And being human means we grieve because we love. And we grieve because we *still* do.

The Mental Toll of Bereavement

The experience of grieving can feel like waking up in the middle of the night, not quite asleep, not quite awake—your body still, but your brain somewhere between a dream and a scream. You fumble for the light switch, but the room you're in isn't familiar. You're not sure how you got here, or how to get out.

That's what grieving feels like.

It's a dislocation of the soul. A fog in the mind that doesn't lift with coffee or rest. One moment, you're folding laundry; the next, you're crying into a shirt you didn't realize still smelled like them. One moment, you're fine, and then you're *not*.

Dante, in his *Divine Comedy*, called Purgatory a mountain that souls must climb to purify their sorrow (Alighieri, 1321/2010). But what he doesn't describe is what it feels like when you're still at the bottom, still in the dark, staring up at something too big to name. That's the mind of the grieving: Stuck between memory and survival, longing and fear, heaven and earth.

Let's talk about what this toll actually looks like—one piece at a time.

Brain Fog and Forgetfulness

You find your keys in the fridge. You open your mouth to speak and forget what you wanted to say. You stare at emails like they're written in another language.

These are all signs of the brain's emergency response system trying to ration your energy. When you're grieving, your body redirects resources to emotional survival, and then attention, memory, and focus take a back seat. Everything slows. You're not "losing it." You're grieving.

This is why even simple tasks such as writing a grocery list, finishing a sentence, or remembering what day it is, can feel insurmountable. The world keeps spinning, but your inner world is frozen in amber.

Permit yourself to forget. To be slow. To pause and start again.

Rumination

Have you ever had a thought that you just couldn't let go of? One that plays in the back of your mind on repeat, until you're not sure whether you're remembering or just stuck in a loop?

Grief has a way of doing that. It circles back to the same moments again and again. The last conversation. The phone call. The things you wish you'd said. The things you wish you hadn't.

These thoughts don't come all at once; they drip in slowly, quietly, until they fill the space around you. They show up when you're doing something ordinary: folding laundry, scrolling your phone, trying to fall asleep.

It's your mind's way of trying to make sense of what doesn't make sense. A quiet, almost frantic attempt to rewrite the ending. To understand. To find something solid in the middle of everything that feels uncertain.

While it can be exhausting, this repetition is part of how we begin to heal. Your heart is processing what your body already knows but can't quite accept.

So, when the thoughts return, and they will, try not to fight them. Let them pass through. Let them say what they need to say. But remember: You don't have to follow them down every path. Not every thought tells the truth.

Disorientation and Derealization

Many grieving people describe a sensation that the world no longer feels *real*. Colors seem muted. Sounds feel distant. You might feel like you're watching your life from outside your body, as if you're underwater or behind glass.

This is called derealization, and it's a protective response. Your nervous system is overwhelmed, and as a result, your brain temporarily detaches, a coping mechanism to manage overload (Mayo Clinic Staff, 2017).

You may lose track of time. You forget how many days have passed, or whether something happened yesterday or last week. It's not just confusion, it's disconnection.

You are not going crazy. You're adapting. Even if you don't feel "in" the world right now, that doesn't mean you won't find your way back.

Anxiety

After a loss, many people begin to fear more loss.

You start noticing every ache, every pain, every unanswered text. Your heart races at small triggers. You feel jumpy, on edge. You fear the next phone call will bring bad news.

This is the body's way of trying to *prevent* more pain. Your system is in high alert, scanning for danger. But it's also exhausting. You might feel like you're holding your breath all the time, just waiting for the next blow.

Grief makes you feel like the world is no longer a safe place. That which happened once can happen again, at any moment. This is a trauma response—and it deserves compassion, not criticism.

Numbness

Sometimes, grief doesn't manifest as sadness. It doesn't come with tears, heartbreak, or rage. Sometimes, it shows up as nothing at all.

A blankness.

You're not crying. You're not angry. You're not even sure what you feel, just that everything is muted. Food has no taste. Music doesn't move you. Time feels heavy and slow. You catch your reflection and barely recognize the person looking back.

This is grief, too. It's the kind that slips beneath the radar, not loud or dramatic, but just as real. Often, it's depression sitting quietly beside your loss. A protective shutdown. The body's way of turning down the emotional volume when it all becomes too much.

Yes, it can be scary. Numbness feels like disconnection from the world, from others, from yourself. You might even wonder if you're broken, or if you've stopped caring altogether.

But you haven't. You're just tired. You've been carrying more than your heart was built to hold, and your system is trying to conserve what little energy you have left.

Guilt and Shame

Grief often brings a shadow: guilt.

Guilt for not doing more. Guilt for surviving. Guilt for laughing. Guilt for feeling *anything* other than grief. And sometimes, when grief is complicated—when the relationship was strained, or the loss brought mixed emotions—there's shame, too.

Shame tells you you're not grieving "right." That you're too emotional. Or not emotional enough. It whispers that your feelings are wrong.

One of my favorite authors, Brené Brown, teaches us that shame thrives in secrecy, silence, and judgment (Brown, 2013). So, let's name it. Guilt is normal. Shame is a liar. And both lose power when we speak them aloud.

When Grief Lives in the Body

We often think of grief as something that happens in the mind, an emotional pain or sadness. But the body doesn't see it that way. To your nervous system, grief isn't "just" a feeling. It's a real threat. Loss signals danger.

When you lose someone or something deeply important, your brain interprets it as a life-threatening event. This triggers your body's ancient survival systems—the same ones that react to physical threats, such as injury or attack. Your body floods with stress hormones like cortisol and adrenaline, putting you into a heightened state of alert.

That's why grief feels so physically intense: your heart races, your chest tightens, your stomach knots, and your muscles tense. You might feel exhausted or restless, unable to sleep or eat. These are not just side effects; they're the body's way of trying to keep you safe.

You may experience:

- **Fatigue or exhaustion:** Even after a full night's sleep.
- **Digestive issues:** Nausea, loss of appetite, or stomach aches.
- **Chest pain or tightness:** A literal ache in the heart.
- **Muscle tension and headaches:** From holding in so much, for so long.
- **Weakened immunity:** Getting sick more often or healing more slowly.

- **Insomnia or vivid dreams:** Disrupted sleep from a racing or overloaded mind.
- **Brain fog or forgetfulness:** Difficulty concentrating or making decisions.

This is your body's grief, speaking in the only language it knows: sensation, tension, stillness, pain.

And it's okay. You're not imagining it. You're not being dramatic. You're responding exactly as a human body is designed to respond when it feels like part of its world has fallen away.

Be gentle with it. Rest. Nourish. Move when you can. Cry when you need to. Healing isn't just emotional, it's physical too.

Self-Love as First Aid

If you've ever been seriously ill and advised to rest, to clear your calendar, to tend gently to your healing body, then you already understand something about grief. Not because grief is a sickness, but because it *demands the same tenderness*. The toll it takes on your body, mind, and spirit is just as real. Invisible, maybe. But just as heavy.

Grief can leave you foggy, fatigued, irritable, and hollow. You may find it hard to eat, sleep, focus, or even breathe fully. And yet, we often expect ourselves to push through it, to carry on as if nothing's happened.

But the healing journey doesn't begin with having all the answers. It begins with *compassion*.

What would it look like to offer yourself the same care you'd give a friend who was hurting? Could you set down the guilt, the "shoulds," the pressure to be okay, and make room for gentleness?

Self-soothing isn't indulgence. It's maintenance. It's what helps regulate a dysregulated nervous system and gives your heart the space to mend.

Here are a few ways to practice it:

- **Grounding rituals:** Sit with your feet on the floor. Hold a warm cup of tea. Light a candle. Do something small that reminds you: *I am here.*
- **Gentle movement:** Stretch. Walk. Breathe deeply. Not to fix anything, but to let your body process what your mind can't.
- **Nourishment:** Eat simple, warm meals—even when you're not hungry. Drink water. Grief is hard work, and your body needs fuel.
- **Permission to rest:** Lie down. Nap. Do nothing without apology. Productivity isn't the measure of your worth right now.
- **Creative release:** Journal. Scribble. Cry to music. Self-expression helps the pain *move*, rather than stay stuck.
- **Sensory comfort:** Wrap up in a soft blanket. Listen to soothing sounds. Be in nature. Surround yourself with calm things that ask nothing of you.

You are not broken, even if everything feels shattered. You are grieving. And grief changes the map—but not the journey.

You're still here. You're still becoming. And that means something tender, and possibly beautiful, is still waiting for you on the other side.

Even if you can't see it yet.

Chapter Exercises

These exercises are not meant to fix your grief. Nothing needs fixing. Instead, they are invitations to feel, reflect, remember, and reconnect. Take your time. Skip the ones that don't call you. Return to them as many times as you need.

The Grief Roll Call

We often don't realize just how many forms of grief we're carrying. Some are loud. Some are quiet. Some haven't even been named.

Prompt: Make a list of every loss you've experienced that still lives inside you. These can include:

- people
- pets
- friendships
- relationships
- homes
- health
- dreams or identities that no longer exist

Label each as "seen" or "unseen." Was your grief acknowledged by others, or did you carry it alone? You may find grief hiding in places you didn't think to look.

Then, write one sentence for each loss that begins with "You mattered because..."

The Missing Scene

Grief often circles around one moment—the last conversation, the goodbye you didn't get, the news you wish you hadn't heard.

Prompt: Write the scene that you wish had happened. Rewrite the ending. Let yourself say what you never got to say. Let them say what you wish you could have heard. This isn't denial, it's care. Your heart remembers what it needed. Give it the space to imagine.

Grief in the Body

Your body remembers loss, even when your mind tries to forget. Let's tune into its wisdom.

Prompt: Sit quietly. Close your eyes. Where does your grief live in your body today? Your throat? Your chest? Your stomach?

Describe it using sensory words: Is it tight, hollow, warm, cold, sharp, buzzing?

Then ask it gently: *What do you need from me today?*

Write down whatever answer comes.

Closing Thoughts

Grief remakes you, moment by moment, breath by breath, whether you want it to or not. And while it may never quite leave, it changes shape. Over time, the sharp edges soften. The weight shifts, and you learn to carry it better.

What we've explored here is just the beginning: A map of the terrain, not the journey itself. The different kinds of loss. The way it rattles the mind, floods the body, and reshapes your days.

But all of it leads to this one, essential truth: Grief is love, transformed. And to grieve is not a sign that you're weak, or broken, or stuck—it's a sign that you loved deeply enough for something to matter.

But what happens in the *very beginning*? When the loss is fresh, and the world turns surreal? When everything is too loud, too quiet, too much, and somehow not enough?

Let's talk about it in the next chapter.

Chapter 2

Shock, Numbness, and the First Waves

Be gentle with yourself, you're doing the best you can.

— Unknown

In the wake of loss, everything can feel surreal. The rules you lived by—the way mornings began, the weight of your footsteps, the rhythm of your conversations—don't apply anymore. You try to make sense of it, to reach back and touch what used to be real, but it's like trying to hold water in your hands. The mind stalls in disbelief. Your body goes through the motions, but your heart is still asking, *"Did this really happen?"*

And here's the part we don't talk about enough: You might not feel what you thought you'd feel. You might not cry. You might feel numb. You might even feel okay. For some, grief doesn't come like a tidal wave; it tiptoes in, slow and strange, and with that comes guilt. *Shouldn't I be more devastated? Why am I functioning when it feels like I shouldn't be?*

There is no one right way to grieve. There is only your way—and even that can change moment to moment. This chapter is a place for that messy beginning. For the fog, the stillness, the moments where everything feels out of joint.

Shock

Generally speaking, shock is the body's way of saying, *"This is too much. I need a minute."*

It's often misunderstood as a fleeting moment of surprise or disbelief. But real shock—the kind that stops you in your tracks and changes how you feel in your body is so much more than that. It's a primal, whole-body response to a moment when your world abruptly stops making sense.

We experience shock in many contexts. The *bad kind*, like when you witness a car crash, get a devastating phone call, or hear a diagnosis that doesn't yet feel real.

As such, in the early moments, you might feel:

- dizzy or detached
- cold or sweaty
- confused, like you're watching life through a screen
- hyperaware of tiny things (a ticking clock, the way the sunlight looks)

That's your survival system flipping every switch at once. Your brain scrambles to make sense of the moment, thinking, *"Is this real? What do I do now?"* while your body tries to conserve energy and prevent overload.

That's the intelligence of the body protecting you from shattering.

When we receive news of a death or experience any life-altering loss, the brain interprets it as a kind of existential trauma (Smith, 2025). Blood rushes to the core. Muscles go slack. Your thoughts feel jumbled, slow, or suspended entirely. You may feel faint or spaced out, or have no memory of what happened in the hours or days that follow.

This is your nervous system sounding the alarm. It doesn't distinguish between physical and emotional emergencies. *Danger is danger.* And grief, especially sudden grief, is one of the most dangerous feelings the human body knows.

The Protective Role of Numbness

So, it's no wonder that the mind's first instinct is to numb us out. It doesn't mean we're in denial. Rather, it means our brain is buying us time.

Time to adjust to a world without that person. Time to recalibrate our internal compass. Time to breathe again before feeling everything that's coming.

We don't always give that kind of shock enough credit. We say things like, "I should be crying," or "I feel like a terrible person for not reacting." But here's the truth: If your mind has gone quiet, if you feel disconnected, if you've floated through your day like a ghost in your own life, you are not broken.

You are in shock. You are surviving.

Think about when you're physically injured, one of the first things a doctor tells you is: "Put some ice on it."

It sounds simple, almost too basic to matter. But that ice pack is doing more than dulling pain; it's also protecting the area. Cold slows down nerve activity, which eases the sharpness of sensation. In other words, the ice gives your body a moment to catch up. A moment to breathe before it fully registers what's happened.

Emotional numbness isn't so different.

We don't choose to feel numb the way we choose to hold a cold pack against a bruise. It just happens. Quietly. Often, in the seconds after your world changes. A car crash. A diagnosis.

And suddenly, you're watching your life from behind glass.

A friend of mine once described her own experience of numbness like this: "*It felt like I was watching myself live my life, but from very far away. I'd see myself walking, talking, answering emails—but it was like I was watching a movie, not actually in it. Like I was sitting in the back row of my own body.*"

That distance she described, that strange feeling of being *here but not quite*, is the mind's way of protecting itself from a reality it can't yet bear.

The Mind's Gentle Escape Hatch

Grief is too big to take in all at once. The body knows this. The nervous system knows this. So sometimes, in the moments after a devastating loss, your brain makes a split-second decision: *We're not ready for all of this right now.* It mutes the sound. It lowers the brightness. It fogs the edges. It does exactly what an ice pack does: It buys you time.

Numbness becomes the only bearable way to move through a world that suddenly feels unsafe, unfamiliar, and unrecognizable.

The Preparations After Loss

Numbness, as we've just explored, can feel like a mercy. It wraps around you like gauze after a deep wound, blunting the pain, slowing the shock, helping you survive the unspeakable.

But here's the cruel paradox: Even as you're floating through the haze of loss, the world demands that you *function*. That you *do things*. That you *get things done*.

While you're still disoriented, perhaps still waiting to wake up from what feels like a bad dream, there's suddenly a list in your hand:

- Call the relatives.
- Sign the paperwork.
- Choose a coffin.
- Write an obituary.
- Plan a service.
- Coordinate travel.
- Prepare food.
- Speak, smile, and thank people for coming.

If that weren't enough, you might also be dealing with financial decisions, medical bills, estate matters, or family tension that rises up like smoke in a burning room. You're making decisions that feel impossibly adult while your heart is still asking, child-like, *"How can they be gone?"*

No one tells you that death brings so much administration. So many logistics. That grief comes with errands.

Yet here you are, torn in two: One part of you grieving, the other part going through the motions. You may still be in denial, still unable to fully say the words out loud, and yet you're picking out hymns or printing programs.

So, how do you do it? How do you cope when your soul wants to collapse, but the world wants you to organize a reception?

Lower the Bar

You do *not* have to be graceful, composed, or endlessly accommodating. You are allowed to forget things. To cry in public. To say, "I don't know," or "Can you help me?"

There is no award for the "Best Grieving Person."

If you can't make the phone calls, delegate. If you can't attend the wake, explain or don't. If you're expected to speak but can't find the words, hand someone a note and let them read it for you.

Your only job is to make it through. That's it. That's enough.

Accept Help

This is not the time to prove your independence. When people ask, "What can I do?" Tell them. Ask them to organize food, answer the door, run errands, or manage the logistics. Let someone else field the texts. Let someone else bring the tissues.

You don't need to earn rest or justify why you're not okay. Grief is work. Let others hold you while you hold the memory of the person you loved.

Build a Pause Into the Chaos

It might feel like the days after a death are a whirlwind, but somewhere in there, try to make space for a moment. A walk. A breath. A moment in the car with music turned down low. A few minutes at the gravesite before everyone else arrives. A chance to just *be*.

You don't need to grieve in public every second. You don't owe anyone performance. Let yourself be still, even if only for a heartbeat.

Expect Strange Emotions and Make Room for Them

You might laugh when you think you shouldn't. You might feel numb when others cry. You might feel resentment, guilt, or even relief. These are not signs that you're doing it wrong. These are signs that you're human.

You're processing a loss while juggling a hundred invisible weights. The fact that you're standing at all is remarkable.

They never tell you how much work awaits you after someone dies, how you'll have to hold your own pain in one hand and a clipboard in the other. But here's the truth: You don't have to do it perfectly. You just have to keep going, one breath, one task, one tear at a time.

And when the last chair is stacked, when the food is packed up, when everyone else goes home, you're still there, holding the ache. Maybe, finally, you can fall apart a little.

Family Dynamics

When Donna's father passed away, she assumed the family would come together, just like in the movies—grief binding them closer, old tensions dissolving in the face of shared heartbreak.

Instead, it felt like everyone scattered in different emotional directions.

Her brother, who'd always been the family clown, went silent. He didn't speak much at the memorial and didn't return texts for weeks. Donna thought he was angry at her until he later admitted he just didn't know what to say.

Her mother, raw and overwhelmed, started micromanaging every detail of the funeral down to the brand of bottled water at the service. When Donna gently suggested they choose one of her dad's favorite songs for the slideshow, her mother snapped: "This isn't about you."

Meanwhile, her cousin Melissa, who hadn't visited her dad in years, suddenly wanted to give a speech, design the program, and critique Donna's eulogy draft, all in the same breath.

It was bewildering. Lonely. And not at all what Donna had expected.

She realized then that everyone was grieving, but not in the same way. Her quiet brother was grieving. Her controlling mother was grieving. Even her overbearing cousin, in her own strange way, was grieving. But instead of feeling united, Donna felt like she was in a room full of strangers who all happened to share the same last name.

That's when she learned: Grief doesn't always bring people closer. Sometimes, it shows you just how differently people love, hurt, and try—imperfectly—to cope.

This is the messy truth: The people you expect to lean on may not know how to hold you. The sibling you thought would step up might check out. The cousin who barely spoke to your dad might suddenly have very strong opinions about the funeral. The aunt who brings casseroles might also bring criticism. And the parent who's "supposed" to be the strongest might unravel right in front of you.

It's disorienting to be grieving and still have to *manage* other people.

Why Grief Stirs Up Old Wounds

When someone dies, it doesn't just bring up sadness. It brings up history. It reactivates old roles, wounds, and unspoken resentments that have lived quietly in the background. Birth order dynamics creep back in. Longstanding tensions resurface. Conversations that should've happened years ago show up late and messy, wearing funeral clothes.

You may find yourself stepping into a caretaking role you never asked for—or feeling unseen, unheard, or misunderstood by the people who are supposed to know you best.

It doesn't mean your family is broken. It means everyone is hurting, and everyone is doing what they know how to do to survive that hurt.

How to Stay Grounded in the Storm

If this is where you are—surrounded by people you love but don't understand, or maybe don't feel safe with—here are a few ways to protect your peace:

- **Give yourself permission to have boundaries:** You don't have to attend every conversation, solve every conflict, or be the emotional referee. You're allowed to say, "I can't have this talk right now," or "I need space."
- **Let people grieve their way:** Even if it looks wrong to you. Even if you wish they'd open up, calm down, or stop making everything about them. Grief is a process, and everyone's process will look different.
- **Be gentle but clear:** If something hurts you, you can name it without blame. "I know we're all raw right now, but when you said that, it felt like…" or "I'm not

in a place to talk about that today." Grief doesn't give anyone a free pass to harm you.
- **Find your anchor:** Maybe it's a friend outside the family, a therapist, a partner, or even a journal. Somewhere, you can exhale without judgment. Somewhere, you can untangle your own feelings without the noise of everyone else's.

Grieving in a Room Full of Grievers

One of the loneliest feelings in the world is standing in a room full of people who loved the same person you did—and still feeling alone.

But despite all the mess, all the differences, all the awkward silences or clashing opinions, there is a thread running through everyone in that room. And that thread is love. Complicated love. Imperfect love, but still love.

Sometimes you have to dig for it. Sometimes it's buried under years of disappointment or dysfunction. But it's there.

And if nothing else, let that thread remind you: You are not the only one missing them.

Staying Grounded

They say time heals all wounds, but what they don't say is how *long* time can take, especially when grief doesn't feel like sadness or anger or heartbreak.

Sometimes, it just feels like *nothing* at all.

You might be in a room full of laughter and feel like a ghost. You might show up to work, go through the motions, answer messages, pay bills, but something inside you remains untouched, unreachable, like your soul is wrapped in cotton wool.

This is what numbness can become: Not just a moment of shock, but a prolonged state of quiet withdrawal. Not a breakdown, but a slow fading out.

When It Lasts Longer Than You Thought

For some people, this phase passes quickly. For others, it lingers. I've known it to stretch on for months, even *years*. And the hardest part is that you can't always tell it's happening, until one day, you look up and realize: *I haven't really felt much of anything in a long time.*

You might wonder: *Is something wrong with me? Have I stopped caring? Am I broken?*

The answer is no. You're not broken. You're protecting yourself.

Numbness is the mind's version of scar tissue, a shield it forms when life becomes too sharp to touch directly. It doesn't mean you're avoiding grief. It means your nervous system is doing its best to keep you functioning.

But even protective mechanisms can start to feel like prisons if they stay too long.

So, how do we stay grounded when grief pulls us up and away from ourselves?

Name the Numbness Without Judging It

Say it out loud. Write it down. Share it with someone you trust: "I feel detached. I feel foggy. I'm not sure I'm even here."

Bringing awareness to the feeling is the first step in loosening its grip. You don't need to fix it. Just witness it with tenderness.

Choose Gentle Contact Points

You don't need to dive headfirst into emotion. Try simply dipping your toes back into the world through small acts of presence:

- Touch something warm or textured.
- Eat something flavorful, even if you're not hungry.
- Step outside and feel the sun or the cold air on your skin.
- Take a shower and notice the water.

These little moments remind your body: *I am still here.*

Create a Daily Grounding Ritual

Something short. Something consistent. You might:

- Sit with your hand over your heart for one minute.
- Light a candle and breathe deeply.
- Listen to a song that doesn't ask too much of you.

These rituals are like anchors when everything else feels adrift.

Practice Gentle Re-Entry

It's okay if you don't feel ready to fully "engage" with life. You can start by connecting to small things: a pet, a plant, a short walk, a line in a poem that stirs something faint but familiar.

Don't wait for big emotion. Just follow the thread and let that guide you back.

Seek Connection Even if You Feel Nothing

Isolation strengthens numbness. Sometimes, the very thing you want to avoid—*other people*—is what helps break the spell. Be with someone. Sit in silence together. Go somewhere where life is happening, even if you're not ready to participate. Let yourself be near it.

Even if you don't feel the warmth yet, just sitting by the fire helps.

Closing Thoughts

This long, stretched-out, and quiet stage can feel endless. But numbness, for all its weight, is not the absence of love. It's what love looks like when it's curled up and waiting to feel safe again.

So don't rush it. Don't shame it. But don't forget that you are allowed to come back to yourself. Whenever you're ready. However slowly it takes.

Chapter 3

Facing Life Without Them

Grief is just love with nowhere to go.

— Jamie Anderson

There comes a moment—quiet, hollow, almost impossible to name—when you realize this is your life now. Not the life you planned. Not the one you imagined growing old into. But a life that still insists on moving forward, breath by breath, even as your heart aches for what is missing.

Whether you've chosen it or not, a new reality has taken shape around you. And ready or not, whether you feel equipped or not, you are being asked to live inside of it. It's an overwhelming request, especially when your days are still stitched together with pain, and your routine has been ruptured in ways both visible and invisible.

Going Back to Normal Without Them

"Time, the healer of all wounds." "Time waits for no one." "Life goes on."

We say these things, we hear these things, and sometimes we even tell them to ourselves, repeating them like a mantra, like a life raft we're hoping might carry us through the unbearable. But in the days following the loss of someone we love, those phrases meant to comfort can feel like a betrayal. Because the truth is, when someone we love dies, the world doesn't stop. Time does march on. But it doesn't do so gently.

What no one tells you is how viscerally aware you become of this movement of time. You notice the clatter of shopping carts at the grocery store, the laugh echoing across a café, a cheerful radio jingle playing in a car that whizzes past. In that moment, something inside you shatters all over again.

How Can the World Just Turn?

How can people still smile? How can the cashier still ask, "How's your day been so far?" as if the earth hasn't cracked wide open beneath your feet?

It's the jarring realization that your worst day, your most painful moment, is just another Tuesday to someone else. The time you spent in hospital waiting rooms, or answering the call you never wanted to come, or sitting numbly on the floor, wondering how this could possibly be real. That time now sits completely unnoticed in the world around you. That's the injustice of loss. The clock keeps ticking, even when your heart feels like it's frozen.

Eventually, far too soon, if you ask anyone who's grieving, you're expected to go back. Back to the inbox, deadlines, and dinner plans. Back to smiling on cue, answering texts, and remembering to take the chicken out of the freezer. But what you're actually going back to is a life that now has a gaping hole in it. No matter how often you used to see them, every day, once a week, or even once a year, their absence is unbearable. Because the fact that they are no longer here and will never be here again is too immense for language, it sits in your chest like a stone.

That permanence is the hardest part. It's not just that they're gone. It's that they will never walk through that door again. Never text you back. Never be a surprise guest at a family gathering or someone you bump into on a rainy Tuesday. That "never again" is what breaks us. That's what makes the idea of *normal life* feel absurd.

Yet, here you are, in the tension of two impossible truths: The world has ended *for you*, but the world has also carried on *without you*. And learning to live inside that contradiction—to carry your love, your longing, and your grief into a life that asks you to function like everything is fine—is the quiet courage no one sees. It's a kind of heroism that doesn't get celebrated, but should. Because choosing to keep showing up in a life that no longer feels whole? That's not "moving on." That's resilience.

You are allowed—no, you are expected to struggle with that. It's not weak. It's not overdramatic. It's the cost of having loved deeply. And you wouldn't trade that love to avoid the pain, even if you could.

So, if today you feel like you can't imagine "going back to normal," let me be the one to tell you: You don't have to. You're not going back. You're going forward. With your grief. With your memories. And with a heart that knows how to love in a world that sometimes breaks it.

Loneliness and Isolation

Nobody really gets it.

When Dan died, Alan lost more than just his best friend; he lost the one person who knew all the versions of him. The reckless teenager. The heartbroken college kid. The guy who hated Christmas music but always sang along with Dan in December anyway.

The day after the funeral, Alan sat on his couch, phone in hand, fingers hovering over Dan's name. He'd just watched a movie they would've both torn apart in hysterics, and without thinking, he reached for his phone to text him. Mid-type, he froze. The number was still there. Dan wasn't.

When he tried to talk about it, to say, "I keep forgetting he's gone," or "I don't know who to be funny with anymore," people nodded politely, but it was clear they didn't get it.

Dan wasn't their best friend. They didn't know about the terrible band they'd tried to start in high school or the road trip where they'd gotten lost for six hours and somehow ended up in a town that smelled like pickles.

People tried to comfort him. They said, "He's in a better place," or "At least you have the memories." One person even said, "It's not like you lost a brother."

But Alan *had* lost a brother. Just not one related by blood.

The hardest part? No one else knew Dan well enough to miss him *properly*. Alan felt like the sole archivist of Dan's existence, the keeper of every inside joke, every embarrassing story, every shade of the person the world never really saw.

Now, he carried all that alone. So, it should come as no surprise, then, that one of the quietest companions of grief is loneliness.

Not the kind you fix with a phone call or a coffee date. Not the kind that lifts when someone sends a kind message or checks in on you. This is the kind of loneliness that aches. The kind that lingers even when you're surrounded by people who love you. The kind that curls up beside you in a crowded room and whispers, They don't get it. Not really.

And they don't. How could they? Some will try—bless them—and you'll be grateful, truly. Their presence is something. However, the absence of understanding, even when unintentional, is also something to consider. It's what makes grief feel like you're living behind glass: Present but removed, visible but unreachable. They're on the outside of it, looking in, trying to comfort you from a place where the air is still breathable. You're on the inside, suffocating on the weight of what you can't say out loud.

Even when you try to put words to it, they fall short. How do you explain a bond that lives in the marrow of your bones? How do you describe the way your world shifted off its axis the moment they were gone? How do you make someone understand that you're not just missing a person—you're missing a piece of yourself?

There is a particular loneliness in grief that has nothing to do with physical solitude. It's a soul-deep aloneness, a sense that no one can truly accompany you through this, not all the way. People can walk alongside you, yes. They can hold space for you, and cry with you, and feed you, and send you voice notes that make you smile through the tears. But no one else is carrying your specific loss. No one else lost exactly what you lost.

That's why, even in the presence of kindness and community, grief can still feel like exile.

So, if you feel lonely, even when people are trying to show up for you, please don't shame yourself for it. That doesn't mean you're ungrateful. That doesn't mean you're closed off or broken. It means you're grieving something real and irreplaceable. And the world doesn't always have the language or rituals to hold that kind of pain the way it deserves to be held.

But you're not truly alone in the loneliness. Not if you name it, not if you give it space, and not if you remember that somewhere. Maybe even right here, many may be reading this and whispering, "Me too."

Creating Your New Life

At some point, after the shock quiets, after the world has moved on and you're left staring at the space where they used to be, you're faced with something that feels almost impossible: Now what?

How do you build a life when it feels like a part of your own has died? How do you keep going when the version of you that existed with them is no longer whole?

This is where grief gets subtle. It stops screaming and starts whispering in your ear: *You have to find a new way to live now.* Not because you want to. Not because you've moved on. But because you're still here, and that matters.

Creating a new life after loss is not about erasing the past; it's not about "getting over" anything. It's about honoring what was by choosing to live fully in what is. It's about becoming a version of yourself that has been broken and lived. A version of yourself that knows deep love, deep loss, and still chooses to wake up and breathe and try again.

Yes, at first, it will feel like pretending. Like putting on a costume and walking through a world that no longer makes sense. That's okay. In the beginning, you're not creating a *new life*; you're simply creating a *rhythm* that helps you survive the next ten minutes. That is more than enough.

But as you start to find your feet again, something begins to shift. Slowly, gently, you begin to recreate yourself. Not in spite of your grief but with it and around it. You start asking new questions:

- What kind of life would honor the love I lost?
- Who am I now, without them?
- What lights are still flickering inside me, waiting to be noticed?

Recreating yourself doesn't mean you abandon the person you were. It means you weave the loss into your becoming. You let it inform the way you love. The way you show up. The way you speak, create, move, and connect. You allow your grief to be a compass, not the whole map, but a powerful part of it.

So, how do you begin to create this new life?

Make Room for Stillness

Grief needs stillness to speak. Take walks without music. Sit in the sun. Journal without a goal. Let your inner voice come forward without the noise of distraction. That voice, the quiet one that speaks in images and feelings, holds the blueprints of who you're becoming.

Reclaim Your Body

Loss lives in the body. So does resilience. Dance, stretch, run, rest. Do something that reminds you that you are still *here*. That you are alive. That your body is a home worth coming back to, even if it feels like grief has changed the locks.

Start a Project

Not to be productive. Not to keep busy. But to *create meaning*. Plant a garden. Paint your memories. Learn to cook the meals they loved. Write letters to them you'll never send. Create something that transforms pain into beauty, even quietly, even clumsily.

Find People Who've Been Through It

Grief is an island only until you meet someone else who's been shipwrecked. Join a support group. Reach out to someone who's walked this path. You don't need to say much. Sometimes, just sitting next to someone who *gets it* is more healing than any advice.

Give Yourself Permission to Feel Joy

This one's the hardest. Because joy initially feels like betrayal. But joy is not a sign that you've forgotten. It's a sign that love is still alive in you. Let joy coexist with sorrow. Let it surprise you. Let it heal you.

Tell a New Story About Yourself

You are no longer just the person you were before the loss. You are someone who has loved, who has hurt, who has *survived*. You don't have to write the whole new story right now. But start a sentence: "I am someone who…" Let it grow from there.

Creating a new life after loss is not a straight line. It's a spiral. You will circle back to the pain over and over. But each time, you'll return with new strength, new perspective, and a new piece of yourself.

This is not about becoming *someone else*. It's about becoming more *yourself* than you've ever been, because you now know what it means to live with open hands and an open heart, even when it hurts.

Chapter Exercises

"The World Kept Turning" Reflection

Pick a regular, ordinary thing you did recently, like washing the dishes, standing in line, or hearing a song on the radio.

Now ask yourself:

- *What did it feel like to be doing this thing in a world without them?*
- *What emotions came up that I didn't have the words for in that moment?*
- *What would I say to them about it if I could?*

This highlights how grief is an integral part of everyday life and how validating your emotional responses can make those moments less alienating.

"The Life We Never Got to Live" Collage

Create a visual or written collage of moments, milestones, or experiences you imagined having with the person you lost.

Then reflect:

- *How can I carry their presence into those experiences if they still happen?*
- *What would they want for me, in the absence of these shared futures?*

Grief is often not just for the person, but for the life you imagined together. Naming that grief is a way of honoring both your love and your pain.

Closing Thoughts

You didn't ask for this grief. But you are becoming someone because of it. And that new life? That's not a betrayal. It's a testament to your love, your courage, your aching persistence to stay alive in a world that now feels different, colder, quieter. The fact that you are still here, still waking up, trying to piece together meaning out of a life that shattered is not a weakness. This is love, in its most resilient form.

You don't move on. You carry. You weave. You integrate. Slowly, without even realizing it, you will begin to grow around the ache. Not because you've forgotten, but because you've remembered so well, so fiercely, that the only thing left to do is to live in a way that honors them.

This chapter has been about finding your footing in a new life you never chose, about facing the ordinary days that feel impossibly hollow, and slowly, painfully, learning how to breathe through them. It's the beginning of a long, tender integration, a soft rebuilding of self in a world that feels permanently altered.

But as you may have already discovered, grief does not always move quietly. It doesn't always whisper. Sometimes, it roars.

And so in the next chapter, we'll sit with one of grief's loudest companions: *anger*. The resentment, the rage, the haunting question: *Why?*

Because even in the most sacred heartbreak, sometimes all you want to do is scream. And you wouldn't be alone in that either.

Chapter 4

Anger, Resentment, and the Why

There is no right way to grieve. There is only your way—and it matters.

— Unknown

It starts with something small. You spill your tea. The barista gets your order wrong. The person in traffic cuts you off, and suddenly it's not just irritation, it's fury. Your jaw clenches. Your eyes sting. You're yelling in your head (or maybe out loud), and somewhere deep down, you know it's not really about the tea or the traffic or the stranger who bumped into you at the store.

It's about what you've lost. It's about what you're carrying. It's about everything you *can't* fix.

Anger in grief often arrives unannounced, wild and sharp. It doesn't ask permission or wait until you're "ready." It sneaks into your voice, your sleep, your body. Sometimes, it makes you feel like a stranger to yourself. But what if it's not something to be ashamed of? What if it's trying to tell you something?

Anger is often seen as the "bad" emotion, the one we should stuff down or hide. But at its core, anger is a signal. It tells us a boundary has been crossed. That something important has been taken. That we are in pain and we don't yet know what to do with it.

In grief, that signal is often blaring.

Because when we lose someone or something we love deeply, the world keeps spinning as if nothing happened. We're left holding a bag of shattered pieces, expected to function as if we're not falling apart. That disconnect alone can be enraging.

Anger can be loud. It can be quiet. It can be messy. But it's never meaningless.

In this chapter, we'll look at what anger really is: Not just a reaction, but a response. Often a cover for more vulnerable emotions like fear, hurt, or helplessness. We'll unpack the resentment that can build, not just toward others, but toward life itself, even toward the person we've lost. And we'll talk about the "why," the endless, looping question that haunts so many of us in the aftermath of loss.

Why did this happen? Why them? Why now? Why me?

We'll explore how to face those questions without getting lost in them, how to name the anger without letting it define us, and how to create space for compassion, for ourselves and for others who may not fully understand what we're going through.

This chapter won't try to extinguish your anger. Instead, it will help you sit with it, listen to it, and find your way through it because anger is not the enemy. It's part of the map. It can point us back to what mattered, what still matters, and what needs to be held gently in order to heal.

Rage

In the landscape of grief, anger is the wildfire that scorches everything in its path. It is sudden, consuming, and often terrifying in its intensity. Yet, it is also completely, heartbreakingly human.

Elisabeth Kübler-Ross, in her foundational work on the five stages of grief, named anger as a natural, even necessary, part of the grieving process (Kübler-Ross, 2005). But what she didn't always emphasize, and what we must talk about here, is just how *raw* that anger can feel. This isn't a neat, tidy emotion. It is not polite or productive. It does not wait for its turn. It slams into you, sometimes out of nowhere, and demands to be felt.

It might sound like:

- Why did this have to happen?
- Where were the doctors?
- Why didn't I say goodbye?
- Why did they leave me?
- Why didn't anyone warn me?
- Why them? Why not someone else?

Or maybe it doesn't sound like anything. Maybe it's just a heat that rises behind your eyes, a clenched jaw at the sound of a cheerful voice, a sick churn in your stomach when the world keeps turning and no one seems to notice your devastation.

Grief, at its core, is a reaction to *powerlessness*. You could not stop it. You could not bargain with time. You could not hold them here. Anger is often the first thing we reach for when we feel that kind of helplessness, because it's something. It makes us feel alive. It gives shape and sound to a pain that is otherwise unspeakable.

Sometimes, the rage is directed outward. At the hospital. The driver. The disease. The people who didn't show up. The ones who say the wrong thing.

Sometimes it's directed inward:

- At yourself, for not seeing the signs.
- For not saying "I love you" one more time.
- For being the one still here.
- This is survivor's guilt in its loudest costume.

Sometimes, this is the one thing few people will admit out loud: It's directed at *them*. The person who died. Because they *left*. Because they promised they wouldn't. Because they were careless, or reckless, or didn't fight hard enough. Even if you know, rationally, it wasn't their fault. The anger still comes. And then, shame arrives right behind it.

But I want you to know that your rage is not shameful. It's sacred. It's the body's way of screaming, "This mattered. They mattered. This is not okay."

Anger is your love dressed in fury.

It doesn't make you cruel or broken. It makes you human. Because when we lose someone we can't live without, we are not only heartbroken, we are *violated*. A natural order has been disrupted. A law of love has been broken. Something you thought was safe has been torn from you, and your soul is rioting against it.

And so, rage flares.

You might feel it while looking at an untouched toothbrush. While watching other people laugh in a restaurant. When the paperwork arrives. When someone says, "They're in a better place." When you see your own reflection and realize that *they are not coming back.*

The injustice of it all becomes unbearable.

This is what people don't talk about enough. That grief is not only sadness, it is protest. Protest against what was taken. Against how fast it happened, against how cruel the world can be.

So, let me say this clearly: You are allowed to rage. You are allowed to scream into pillows and curse the sky and cry until your throat is raw. You are allowed to feel like a volcano of fury and heartbreak all at once.

Because this is what love looks like when it has nowhere to go.

Let it move through you. Not because it will fix anything, but because trying to swallow it down will destroy you. Let your rage speak. Let it punch the silence. Let it name what was lost, and what was stolen, and how completely powerless you felt to stop any of it.

Resentment

If rage is the thunderclap of grief, resentment is the slow, silent drip that erodes the foundation beneath you. It's quieter than anger, more socially acceptable, and far harder to admit. But it is no less devastating. In many ways, it's even more corrosive, because it wears the mask of logic, of control, of detachment. Yet underneath, it's pure heartbreak.

Resentment often slips in after rage has exhausted itself. When the shouting has stopped, and all you're left with is a hollow ache and the cruel realization that the world is still turning without the person you loved, that's when resentment starts to grow. You don't invite it. But it arrives anyway.

You notice it in strange moments when:

- Watching a mother hug her child, and feeling like someone just punched you in the chest.
- Seeing a couple laughing in the grocery store, and having to leave your cart behind just to catch your breath.
- Listening to someone complain about trivial things and wanting to scream, "*Do you even know how lucky you are?*"

It's not that you *want* anyone else to suffer. But your pain feels so large, so invisible, so *unshared*, that everyone else's normalcy feels like a slap in the face.

You begin to resent their joy. Their innocence. Their *untouchedness*. You resent the fact that they still have what you've lost. That they don't *know*. That maybe they *never will*.

If you were a person of faith before the loss, you might begin to feel the most dangerous resentment of all: the kind that is pointed *upward*. Toward God. The universe. Fate. Life itself.

You might think:

- Why would a loving God allow this?
- Why did you take them and not me?

- Why didn't you save them? Answer me, warn me?
- What kind of God sits silently while a heart breaks this way?

You might look at your faith, not just religious, but the quiet trust you had in the order of things, and realize it's been shattered. With that shattering comes bitterness. Because betrayal isn't just personal, it can be cosmic.

This is the dark truth no one wants to say out loud: *You can love God and still resent Him.* You can believe in something bigger and still feel furious that it allowed something so small and precious to be taken.

Resentment happens when your love has nowhere to land and your questions have no answers. It's what fills the silence when comfort doesn't come.

And it's okay to name it.

It doesn't mean you're cruel or ungrateful or faithless. It means you're grieving. Deeply. Honestly.

It means you're *still* holding on to the idea that things were supposed to be different, that life was supposed to be kinder, that someone, somewhere, should have stepped in.

The hard and unvarnished truth is that resentment is not a flaw in your character. It's a flag planted in the soil of loss that says, "This mattered. This hurt. This should never have happened."

But left unacknowledged, resentment curdles. It isolates. It whispers things like "No one understands," and "Everyone else gets to be happy except me." It can build walls so tall around your grief that not even love can get in.

So, what do you do?

You speak it. You say, "Yes, I feel bitter today." You say, "Yes, I hate that people still have what I've lost." You say, "Yes, I resent the silence of the universe." Then, slowly, you let that resentment be met with gentleness, with community, with truth. The truth is that grief is a fire, and no one walks through it clean. That resentment isn't who you are; it's a wound that hasn't yet been tended to.

How to Handle the Anger

Elisabeth Kübler-Ross identified anger as the second stage of grief, following denial. But it doesn't follow a schedule (Tyrrell et al., 2023). It might come early or late, or loop back around when you thought you were "done." You may feel rage flare up years after the loss, triggered by a smell, a milestone, or a random Tuesday. That doesn't mean you're broken. It means you're grieving.

So, how do you live with anger that feels volcanic? That simmers just beneath your skin or erupts when you least expect it?

Let's walk through this together.

Name It Without Shame

The first step in handling grief-induced anger is to *acknowledge it*. Without censoring yourself. Without apologizing.

Say it:

- I'm angry they died.
- I'm angry I didn't get more time.
- I'm angry at the doctors, at myself, at God.
- I'm angry that life just keeps going like nothing happened.

- I'm angry that they didn't take better care of themselves.
- I'm angry that I *have* to be angry.

All of it is valid. All of it is grief trying to find oxygen.

Move It Through Your Body

Anger is visceral. It doesn't just live in your mind; it settles in your muscles, your jaw, your gut. That means it often needs a *physical* outlet, not just a mental one.

You can:

- Go for a run or walk somewhere you can breathe and be loud.
- Scream into a pillow or the ocean or the car.
- Hit something safe, such as a punching bag, a mattress, or a pile of soft cushions.
- Try cathartic writing by pouring your fury onto the page without holding back.
- Do grounding movements like yoga or stretching, letting the emotion pass *through*, and not getting stuck *in* it.

Releasing anger physically doesn't mean you're out of control. It means you're tending to your nervous system. You're making space for the storm to pass.

Write A Rage Letter. Burn It If You Must

Sit down and write a letter to the person you lost, or to the system, the doctor, the world, the God you feel betrayed by. Let the rage be honest and unedited.

Say the things you feel like you're not *supposed* to say:

- Why didn't you fight harder?
- Why did you leave me?
- You promised you'd always be here.
- I hate this. I hate you. I hate what this has done to me.

Then? Burn it. Rip it up. Shred it. Or keep it tucked away in a drawer like a secret prayer. There's power in honoring emotions that were never allowed to speak.

Give It a Shape. Give It a Voice

Sometimes anger softens when it's seen. Try drawing it. Sculpting it. Painting it. If it were a color, what color would it be? If it were an animal, what would it sound like?

By externalizing the anger—giving it texture, temperature, voice—you make it something you can *relate* to, instead of something you fear or suppress.

You can ask:

- What do you need me to know?
- What are you protecting me from?
- What part of me are you speaking for?

Because often, underneath the rage is a younger, softer part of you that is scared, hurt, abandoned, desperate to make sense of the senseless. That part needs compassion, not control.

Talk to Someone Who Won't Flinch

Not everyone can hold your anger. Some people will try to talk you out of it. Or fix it. Or redirect it to gratitude. Avoid them, for now.

Seek out those who understand that anger is a form of *love, trying to survive*. That rage is not a tantrum but a testimony to how much this person meant to you.

This might be:

- a grief counselor or therapist who can help you unpack what's underneath.
- a friend who has lost someone and gets it without needing you to explain.
- a support group where people won't blink at your heartbreak.

You don't need answers. You need space. Safe, brave space where your anger can breathe.

Know It Won't Last Forever, But It Deserves Its Time

Anger can feel endless when you're in it. But it's not. It's a wave. And waves move. They rise, crest, and eventually break.

Let it pass through you. Don't rush it. Don't fear it. Don't judge yourself for it.

When the wave recedes, it will leave behind clarity. You'll begin to see the *real* shape of your grief. And in that shape, there is love.

Chapter Exercise

Anger as a Creature

Prompt: Imagine your anger is a living being. Not a monster, but a creature with purpose—here to protect you, speak for you, and remind you that you are still alive.

Instructions:

1. On a piece of paper, draw or describe this creature. Give it a name. A voice. A size. A smell. A color.
2. Ask it: *"Why are you here?"*
3. Let it answer in its own voice.
4. Then ask: *"What do you want me to know?"*
5. Write what it says, word for word.

Why it helps: When we personify emotions, we create distance, not to detach from them, but to listen more clearly. Anger becomes less of a threat and more of a companion. One that, surprisingly, often points the way toward healing.

Closing Thoughts

If you've made it this far, I want to say something simple and true: I'm proud of you. This chapter wasn't easy. Anger never is.

We're taught to hide it. Taught to fear it. Taught to shame ourselves for it. But in grief, anger is not only expected, it's necessary. It is your nervous system's primal alarm that says, *"Something precious has been lost. This is not okay."*

And it's not. It's not okay that they're gone. It's not okay that you didn't get more time. It's not okay that the world keeps turning while you're standing in the wreckage.

But your anger is not a flaw. It's a *flare*—bright, searing, impossible to ignore. It's your love, screaming through the void. It says, "This mattered. *They* mattered. And I am not the same."

If you can let it speak, without letting it harm, anger becomes a strange kind of torch. Not one that burns everything down, but one that lights the way forward. Because beneath the fury, what you'll almost always find is grief. And beneath that? *Love.*

As we move into the next chapter, we enter another complicated corner of grief: guilt and bargaining. The *"If onlys."* The *"I should have knowns."* The aching wish to trade anything, everything, for just one more day, one more word, one more chance to make it right.

Guilt whispers that we failed. Bargaining begs for a loophole. Together, they spin a storm of what-ifs and why-didn'ts and maybe-if-I-had.

But just like with anger, we're going to face these feelings, not to silence them but to understand them. To find the truth beneath their noise.

Chapter 5

Guilt and Bargaining

What we have once enjoyed deeply we can never lose. All that we love deeply becomes a part of us.

— Helen Keller

Psychiatrist Elisabeth Kübler-Ross, best known for her groundbreaking work on death and dying, observed these patterns in terminally ill patients (Kübler-Ross, 2005). Her five-stage model of denial, anger, bargaining, depression, and acceptance wasn't meant to be a checklist, but rather a way to describe the emotional landscape she witnessed again and again. Bargaining, she noted, often took the form of silent deals with a higher power: *If I recover, I'll change. I'll be better. I'll make it right.*

That instinct of desperate negotiation in the face of something unthinkable is not exclusive to those confronting their own mortality. It shows up just as fiercely in those of us left behind.

When you're grieving, you may find yourself rewriting the story: *If I hadn't said that. If I had called more often. If I'd noticed the signs. If I'd made them stay home that day.* These are not just thoughts. They are echoes of guilt, sharp and heavy.

Guilt, unlike some of the more visible emotions, can be deceptively quiet. It hides behind "what-ifs" and "should-haves." It plays over and over like a background track in your mind. It can make you believe that somehow, you failed. That you should have known. Should have done more. It should have been different.

But grief often turns us against ourselves before we've even had a chance to process the loss. The guilt isn't proof that you did something wrong. It's proof that you loved deeply and are struggling to make sense of a world without them.

If you let it, guilt can consume you. It can whisper that healing is betrayal, that joy is disloyalty, that forgiveness—especially the kind you owe yourself—is too much to ask for.

This chapter is here to challenge that voice.

We'll walk through the bargaining stage and its endless internal negotiations. We'll name the guilt and look at where it comes from. Then, we'll start the delicate work of letting go, not of love, not of memory, but of the illusion that you could have controlled something that was never yours to control.

Because you deserve peace. Because love and loss are not opposites. Because, as Helen Keller reminded us, what you loved deeply is still with you. Even now.

Guilt

The last conversation Lorraine had with her husband was a fight. Not a dramatic, stormy kind of fight. It was the kind of petty spat every couple has when they're tired, rushed, and navigating the small negotiations of everyday life. Something about the dishes. Or maybe it was laundry. Or who was supposed to pick up milk on the way home? Honestly, she doesn't even remember what started it, just that it ended badly. He'd grabbed his keys, said something clipped, and walked out the door for work. She hadn't kissed him goodbye. She hadn't said, "I love you." She hadn't even looked up from the mess of her morning routine.

He never made it home. Not that night. Not ever again.

Now, Lorraine replays that conversation more than any other memory. Not their wedding vows. Not their first kiss. Not the way he held her hand when they got the news about the pregnancy. No—what plays like a skipping record is that ordinary morning, and the ordinary fight, about ordinary chores.

Tell me honestly: How often do you remember those little squabbles about dishes, or bins, or who left the car on empty? Hardly ever, right? They blow over. That's how marriage works: You argue, you move on, you make dinner together that night. But Lorraine never got to move on. That was the last moment. That insignificant exchange, a throwaway part of the background noise of love, became *everything*. It became the summary of their final chapter.

Now she wonders, obsessively: *Did he think I was angry with him? Did he think that's how I really felt? Was that the note our love ended on?*

Guilt, when it enters the room, doesn't knock. It's not always logical. It doesn't care that the last words you said weren't cruel, just curt. It doesn't care that people fight; it was just one of those days. It comes in anyway. It sits next to you in the silence. It whispers, *You could have been kinder. You should have known. You should have said something else.*

One of the most brutal truths about grief is this: Guilt can follow you around at any point in the process. It doesn't always show up right away. Sometimes you think you're making peace, and then a memory blindsides you—something you did, or didn't do—and suddenly you're drowning again.

There are so many varieties of guilt that grief awakens.

- There's the guilt about your last interaction.
- The things you never said.
- The apologies you owed but never gave.
- The time you snapped instead of listened.
- The feeling that somehow, you should have seen it coming. Should have stopped it. Saved them.

Then there's the strangest guilt of all: The guilt of living. You will find yourself doing something ordinary like eating a sandwich, laughing at a joke, or taking a walk in the sun, and suddenly feel like you're committing a betrayal. How dare you enjoy this moment when they are gone? You'll think: *They will never feel the sun on their face again, and here I am going on as if the world is still turning.*

You will feel guilty for still being here when they are not.

You may even feel guilty on behalf of others: *Their parents. Their kids. Their friends. Am I grieving hard enough? Am I allowed to grieve this much? Am I grieving too little?*

And it won't come in one neat chapter. It won't move through you in order, tidy, and manageable. No grief or guilt comes in *episodes*. It's a recurring storm, and just when you think it's passed, the sky darkens again.

What Guilt Really Is

Guilt, at its core, is the ache of responsibility with nowhere to go. It's the belief that we should have been able to rewrite what was never in our hands. It comes from our deep longing for control, for some way to make sense of the senseless. So, we turn inward. We think: *If I had only... then maybe...* It's the mind's way of searching for agency in a moment of total powerlessness.

And what does it *feel* like?

It feels like a pit in your stomach that won't leave. It feels like a question mark after every memory. It feels like a courtroom in your head, replaying evidence on loop. It feels like regret laced with shame and dressed in the clothes of love. It feels like you're being punished for surviving.

Guilt is cruel because it disguises itself as love, twisted and sharp-edged, but love all the same. You feel guilty because you loved them. Because you still do. Because part of you believes that loving them meant you should have done more, been more, known more, that you owed them a perfect goodbye.

But the truth? No goodbye will ever feel perfect. No life is wrapped up neatly in a bow. The messiness of being human means we leave behind crumbs, not clean endings. You are not guilty. You are grieving.

You are human. That matters more than perfection ever could.

Guilt of Moving On

If guilt is the shadow that lingers after loss, then perhaps the heaviest part of that shadow falls when you begin to move forward.

Because eventually, whether you want to or not, life does go on.

At first, it's in tiny ways. You smile at something someone says, and the sound of your own laughter shocks you. You watch a movie and realize halfway through you haven't thought about them for nearly an hour. You cook dinner and don't set a second plate. You wake up and, God help you, you feel okay.

With each of these moments, something aches. It's the guilt of healing. The guilt of continuing. The guilt of not being wrecked every single day.

This kind of guilt doesn't always announce itself. It doesn't scream. It's more like a subtle nausea, a feeling that something is wrong with you for not hurting enough. It whispers: Have you forgotten them? How could you be okay when they're not here?

There's guilt in remembering too little. But there's also guilt in remembering too much.

Sometimes you'll catch yourself thinking, What was their voice like again? *Did they always laugh like that? Was that story really the way it happened?* And you'll panic. Because what kind of person forgets these things? What kind of love loses details?

You'll feel like a traitor to your memory. You'll think, *if I were still truly grieving, I would remember everything*. But grief is not a test of devotion. And forgetting is not betrayal. It's biology. It's mercy. It's your mind doing what it must to help you survive.

Still, the shame of forgetting can be devastating. Then comes the other kind of guilt—the guilt of loving again, of building something new.

Maybe it's a new relationship. Maybe it's just a day when you felt light on your feet. Maybe you went a whole morning without crying. Or you met someone who made you feel seen again. In those moments, even joy can feel like desecration.

People will tell you it's okay to move on. But they don't tell you how heavy it can feel to do so. They don't tell you how you might cry harder after a good day than you do after a bad one. They don't tell you that the better you feel, the worse you might feel about feeling better.

Yet, moving forward does not mean moving on.

You do not leave them behind when you start to rebuild your life. You carry them with you. The version of you that existed with them will always be etched into the foundation of who you are now becoming. The love you shared doesn't vanish when you smile again. It evolves. It integrates. It becomes a quiet part of your strength.

Yes, you may forget some things. Yes, you may find joy again. Yes, you may even fall in love again.

And no, none of that means you didn't love them with your whole heart. It means you're still here. Still human. Still living.

Grief doesn't ask us to stop living. It asks us to live honestly, with the complexity of joy braided into pain, memory threaded through movement, guilt held in one hand and grace in the other.

To move forward is not to abandon. It is to honor what was by allowing yourself to become what still can be.

Bargaining

If guilt is the echo of what we think we *should* have done, then bargaining is the desperate attempt to undo what's already been done.

It begins quietly, like a whisper in the dark: *If I'm good, will you bring them back? If I had just done that one thing differently, maybe this wouldn't have happened. If I promise to never complain again, will you make it stop hurting?*

Bargaining is a form of grief logic, not rational, but utterly human. It's our brain trying to buy time with the currency of our own suffering. It's the emotional equivalent of rewinding a tape over and over, trying to find the one scene where, if we just say the right line or make the right choice, everything turns out okay.

We bargain with God. We bargain with fate. We bargain with ourselves. We bargain with the past, as if it were still taking offers.

We tell ourselves stories. Rewritten scripts. Alternate endings. *If I hadn't let them drive. If I'd taken them to the doctor sooner. If I had told them how much I loved them that day.*

When there's no one left to negotiate with, we bargain with memory. We replay conversations, scan text messages, scroll through photos, searching for clues that might grant us some illusion of control, something we missed, something we might still fix if we just suffer enough.

This is the cruel magic trick of bargaining: It offers hope, but it's not real hope. It's a loop. A trap. A painful, compulsive ritual that tries to barter with time and rewrite reality through sheer willpower.

But here's what's often hiding under the surface of bargaining: helplessness. Fear. The unbearable fact that this *thing*—this loss, this grief, this breaking—happened beyond your control. Bargaining steps in and says, *If you just had more power, more awareness, more goodness... You could have stopped it.* And in that, it convinces you that your pain is your penance.

It's not.

You are not being punished. You are not at fault. You are not powerful enough to have changed what happened, not because you were weak or inattentive or unloving, but because death, illness, accident, *and* time, these things are not within our grasp. They never were.

Still, bargaining lingers. It sneaks into the quiet moments, when you're brushing your teeth, when you're staring at the ceiling at 2 a.m., when you're lighting a candle and whispering a prayer you're not sure you believe in anymore. You'll think: *Take something else instead. Anything. Just not this. Just not them.*

Bargaining is not wrong. It's not a mistake. It's a part of grief's strange choreography, one step in a dance you didn't ask to learn. It shows that you are trying to hold onto meaning in a world that suddenly makes none. That your love is still searching for a way to matter, for a way to change the ending.

But eventually, even bargaining runs out of breath. And in its place, often, comes silence. A silence that feels like surrender. Like collapse. Like depression.

But—and this is important—it's not the end. It's the beginning of learning to live with what *is* instead of what *could have been*. It's the moment when your pain stops bargaining and starts grieving.

That's not failure. That's not giving up. That's you, beginning to mourn honestly.

So, if you're still making impossible deals in your mind, be gentle with yourself. Don't rush it. Don't shame yourself for wanting the impossible. That's what love does: It imagines a world where the people we love never leave. That's not wrong. It's beautiful. It's loyal.

But, when you're ready, you can begin the quiet shift from bargaining to being. From pleading to grieving. From *If only...* to *Even though...*

Even though they're gone, I still carry them. Even though I couldn't save them, I can honor them. Even though I would give anything to change the ending, I can still write a life that includes their memory.

You don't have to make peace with the loss all at once. But you can stop bargaining with the past. You can start being here: In the truth, in the pain, in the love that still remains.

Chapter Exercise

This exercise invites you to compassionately name the guilt and bargaining thoughts that have been haunting you, and then gently begin the process of shifting from imagined responsibility to self-forgiveness and truth.

Step 1: Write Your "If Only" Statements

Find a quiet space. With pen and paper (or in a private note on your phone), write down as many "If only..." or "I should have..." thoughts as come to mind. Don't censor or correct them. Let them pour out, raw and unfiltered. These may sound like:

- If only I had called that day...
- If only I had told them I loved them one more time...
- I should have noticed something was wrong...
- I should have done more...

Let these sentences show you where your heart still hurts. This part may bring tears—let it. You're not doing this to dwell. You're doing this to be honest about the ache.

Step 2: Speak to the Guilt

Choose one or two of the strongest guilt statements and write a letter to yourself from a place of understanding, not blame. Imagine you are writing to a friend who feels this way. Say what you wish someone had said to you.

Use phrases like:

- You couldn't have known.
- That day was ordinary because you didn't know it would be the last.
- You loved them in thousands of ways. This one moment does not define your love.
- You are human. You were doing your best with the information you had.

Read your words aloud to yourself. Let them land.

Step 3: Rewriting the Script With "Even Though"

Now begin transforming the narrative—not to erase the pain, but to integrate truth and tenderness. Start a new list. Each line begins with "Even though…" and continues with a truth you are willing to try believing. Some examples:

- Even though I didn't say goodbye, they knew I loved them.
- Even though I can't change what happened, I can carry it forward with love.
- Even though I feel broken, I am learning to be gentle with myself.
- Even though I wish I had done more, I did what I could at the time.

Let the "Even though…" statements be your bridge from guilt to grace.

Step 4: A Final Statement to Keep

Write one sentence to yourself, one truth you want to remember, on a sticky note, a card, or a piece of paper you can carry with you. Something like:

- *They are gone, but the love is not.*
- *I am allowed to heal.*
- *Forgiving myself is also a form of honoring them.*

Let it become your quiet mantra when the guilt returns.

Closing Thoughts

Guilt and bargaining are some of grief's most private chambers. They're not always loud. They don't always look like mourners from the outside. But inside, they echo, replaying conversations, rewriting the past, grasping for control in a world that no longer makes sense.

If you've found yourself stuck in a loop of "what ifs," know this: You are not broken, and you are not alone. These thoughts do not mean you failed; they mean you loved. Deeply. Fiercely. Fully. And now, your mind is trying to make sense of something that defies logic.

You are allowed to forgive yourself for being human. For not knowing. For saying the wrong thing, or not saying the thing you wish you had. You are allowed to grieve imperfectly. There is no version of you—no timeline, no scenario—where the loss would have felt right or fair.

What matters now isn't whether you could have changed the ending. It's how you carry the story forward.

Bargaining says, *"If only."* Guilt says, *"It's my fault."* But healing begins when you whisper back, *"Even though..."*

Even though I couldn't stop this, I can still choose how to honor it. Even though my heart is fractured, I am still capable of love. Even though I would give anything to change the past, I can still shape what comes next.

That shaping begins in the earliest, most bewildering stage of grief, the one that comes before clarity, before rituals, before anything feels remotely okay.

In the next chapter, we'll step into that space together.

We'll talk about the first raw days and weeks after a loss—the emotional shock, the fog, the detachment, the heaviness that settles into the body and mind. It's the part of the journey that no one prepares you for: When the world moves on, but you're still frozen at the moment everything changed.

Chapter 6

After the Storm-Tools for Gentle Healing

> *The reality is that you will grieve forever. You will not 'get over' the loss... You will learn to live with it. You will heal and you will rebuild yourself around the loss you have suffered.*
>
> — Elisabeth Kübler-Ross and David Kessler

You will grieve forever. What a word. Forever. We usually reserve it for love stories and vows, for things we *choose*, not for pain we never asked for. We speak of "forever homes," of "forever people," of dreams that will last us a lifetime. But when grief attaches itself to forever, it becomes a kind of exile. A sentence without end. Yet, that is the truth we must somehow carry: That this ache, this absence, will echo through all our days.

We want grief to come with a finish line. We crave a set of steps, a spiritual checklist. Something that tells us: *If you do these things, your loved one will return. Or at least, the worst of the sorrow will lift.* How much easier it would be if grief were like a quest with an end: Endure five years, complete ten acts of kindness, light a candle every day, and then, somehow, you'll be rewarded. Maybe they'll visit you in a dream. Maybe you'll get a message. Maybe something. Anything.

But the cold, dark permanence of *forever* stretches out in front of us, and we are forced to confront the terrifying possibility that this pain won't end, it will only change. It's the same kind of fear you might feel standing at the edge of a vast, black ocean at night: no light, no compass, no promise of land. Just you, your loss, and the endless tide of time.

Still, the pieces need to be picked up.

The storm may never fully pass, but moments of calm *do* arrive. Like a stillness after heavy rain, or a sudden shaft of sunlight through dark clouds, healing often comes quietly and subtly, asking nothing, promising little, but offering enough to help us take the next breath.

In this chapter, we'll begin where the dust hasn't even settled— the earliest stage of grief, when everything feels fragile, surreal, and impossibly heavy. This is the time *after the storm* but before anything makes sense again: the weeks after the funeral, when the casseroles stop arriving and the world assumes you've started to "move on," while inside you still feel hollow, suspended, and shell-shocked.

We'll explore what it means to survive those first bewildering days: How to lower the bar of expectation, how to hold space for your own strange and shifting emotions. You'll find tools for managing the chaos, grounding exercises for when the floor feels unsteady, and reminders that you are not doing this wrong, because there *is* no wrong way to grieve.

The Emotional Storm

Grief doesn't always announce itself the way we expect. It doesn't always begin with tears. Sometimes, it starts with silence. With shock. With a surreal, floating feeling like you're watching your life from behind glass. People might be hugging you, saying "I'm so sorry," and all you can think is: *This doesn't feel real.*

That's not just your imagination; it's your brain's way of protecting you.

When you lose someone important, the nervous system goes into emergency mode. Your body interprets the event as a kind of trauma, even if the loss was expected. It floods you with stress hormones, dulls your emotional pain receptors, and creates a sense of detachment so you can get through the impossible without completely breaking down.

This is why, in the early days or weeks after a loss, many people describe feeling like they're moving through a dream or a nightmare. Time doesn't behave the way it used to. Some hours drag. Others vanish. You may forget what day it is, stare at your phone for minutes without knowing what you meant to do, or catch yourself picking up the phone to call them before remembering they're gone.

This is the surreal fog of early grief, and it's normal.

Riding the Rollercoaster

Grief isn't tidy. It doesn't move in gentle, predictable stages. Instead, it comes in waves—rushing, receding, and slamming back again when you least expect it. One moment, you might be staring out the window, unable to feel anything. Next, you're sobbing over a cereal box in the grocery store because it was your favorite.

This is what we sometimes call the *grief storm*. It's the disorienting, unsteady period where your emotional states can swing wildly from one moment to the next:

- You might feel completely numb one day, and inconsolably devastated the next.
- You might laugh at a memory, only to feel guilty for smiling minutes later.
- You might want to be surrounded by people, until you actually are, and all you want is to be alone.

There is nothing wrong with you. This chaos *is* grief. The emotional whiplash is your mind trying to make sense of something that can't be made sense of. The world has shifted on its axis, and your body, heart, and mind are scrambling to find balance again.

Why Everything Feels Unreal

The surreal feeling, often described as being "outside of your body" or "numb," is part of what psychologists call derealization and depersonalization. It's a coping mechanism that kicks in when your brain is overwhelmed by stress.

In these moments, you may find yourself thinking:

- *It's like I'm watching a movie.*
- *I keep expecting them to walk through the door.*
- *I can't believe this actually happened.*

This doesn't mean you're broken or in denial. It means your brain is trying to protect you from a reality too painful to absorb all at once. And so, it lets the truth in piece by piece, in doses. You feel numb, or robotic, or "weird," and then out of nowhere, something crashes through the surface: a scent, a photo, a voicemail you forgot to delete, and the truth hits like a wave.

It's okay if that wave takes you down for a while. It's okay if it knocks the breath out of you. Let it.

You Are Not Going Crazy

It's important to say this plainly: You are not going crazy.

If you feel like you're losing your grip, if you're afraid that this fog will never lift or that the tears will never stop, or that the numbness is permanent. Breathe. These are natural responses to unnatural events. Your body and mind are adapting to a world without someone you loved in it.

The truth is, nothing feels real because something is missing that *should* be there.

Grief is not linear. It's a spiral staircase, and in the emotional storm, it's okay to sit down on one of the steps and rest.

Let the storm rage. You're not expected to control it. Just to stay with yourself through it.

And eventually, the fog will lift, just enough to see one small thing clearly. Then another. Then another. That's where healing begins.

What Can Help

In these first days, sometimes even the first weeks, grief can feel less like an emotion and more like a full-body state. It sits in your bones, in your skin, in your breath. Your sleep is disturbed. Your appetite disappears or becomes insatiable. Time stretches and collapses in strange ways. You might feel like you're outside of your body, watching the world carry on as if nothing has happened.

The early days are not the time for "moving on." It's not the time for deep insights or lessons or even hope. It's about surviving. Minute by minute. Hour by hour. Breath by breath.

Lower the Bar: Survival Is Enough

The single most important thing to know right now? You are not expected to be "functional." You are not a machine that needs to keep humming. You are a human being with a broken heart, and that is sacred territory.

If all you did today was open your eyes and blink into the light, that is enough.

If you made it from the bed to the couch, or simply pulled the blanket tighter around your shoulders, that is enough. If you forgot to eat, forgot what day it is, stared at your phone until the screen dimmed, or cried so hard your chest physically ached, that is still enough.

This moment in grief is not about thriving. It's not about insight, growth, or rising from the ashes. That comes later. Maybe. Right now, this is survival work, and it is holy.

Grief is not a performance. You don't get extra points for holding it together. This is not an audition for sainthood. This is triage. This is rescue. This is the part where you wrap your arms around yourself and say: "I don't have to be okay. I just have to stay."

Imagine someone you love has just been in an accident. You wouldn't hand them a to-do list. You wouldn't ask them to smile more. You'd sit next to them. You'd make tea. You'd keep the lights low and speak softly.

So, be that person for yourself.

Anchor Yourself in Small Routines

Grief untethers you. You lose your sense of place, time, and even identity. That's why small, simple routines, however imperfect, can act as anchors.

Think of:

- Making a cup of tea at the same time every morning.
- Opening the window to let in fresh air.
- Taking a short walk around the block, even if you don't want to.
- Writing a few lines in a notebook each night.

These aren't tasks to "fix" your grief. They're gentle rituals that remind your body: *I'm still here. I'm still alive. There is still a rhythm to this world.*

You don't need a full routine. Just one or two touchpoints that bring even the faintest sense of grounding.

Let Others Help You (Even When You Don't Know What You Need)

One of the cruelest ironies of grief is that you often feel least capable of asking for help when you need it most.

I once heard a woman describe how, after her brother died, a neighbor knocked on the door and asked, "What do you need?" She blinked at her blankly and said, "I don't know. Air?" The neighbor nodded and came back 20 minutes later with a loaf of bread and three scented candles. "I didn't know what air looked like," she said. "But this is what I would want if I couldn't breathe."

That's the kind of help that matters, not grand gestures, but humble ones. Human ones.

So, when people offer, say yes, even if you don't know what you're saying yes to. Let them bring you soup that you might not even eat. Let them sit beside you while you scroll through old photos and cry. Let them take your laundry, your children, or your to-do list and just hold something for you.

You don't need to explain yourself. You don't need to be cheerful, tidy, or grateful. You are not a host. You are someone whose world just cracked open and letting others care for you, even awkwardly, is part of how you survive.

Cry. Scream. Sleep. Repeat.

There is no "right" way to feel grief. Some people cry constantly. Others go numb. Some rage. Some laugh at the worst moments. Some sleep all day. Some can't sleep at all.

All of it is valid.

Let your body lead. If the tears come, let them. If you need to scream into a pillow, do it. If your body demands sleep, surrender to it.

Grief is physical. It moves through us like weather—stormy, unpredictable, impossible to control. The more you let it move, the less likely it is to get stuck.

Avoid Big Decisions (Unless You Absolutely Have To)

Imagine for a second that you've just survived a shipwreck. You're cold, soaked to the bone, clinging to a splintered piece of wood in open water. The sky is spinning. Your ears are ringing. Someone swims up and says, "Quick—make a decision about your mortgage!"

Absurd, right?

Yet, in the aftermath of profound loss, we so often pressure ourselves to make life-altering choices. Sell the house, quit the job, end the relationship, start over completely. Why? Because we want something to *control* in a world that suddenly feels unrecognizable. We think: *Maybe if I just change everything, this hurt won't follow me.*

But early grief is not clarity. It's not wisdom. It's survival mode. The brain fog, the emotional vertigo, the impulse to tear down and rebuild your life, it's all part of the storm.

This is not the time to start a new chapter. It's time to wrap yourself in a blanket and wait out the rain.

If a decision can wait, let it. Don't rush to donate your clothes or leave the home you shared, or send a furious email to your boss, your sister, or your future self. Not yet. These decisions will still be there tomorrow and the next day and the day after that. There is no deadline on healing.

If something *can't* wait? If life forces your hand? Then don't go it alone. Let someone steady stand beside you. Someone who isn't caught in the same storm. Let them hold the map while you take a breath.

Take Breaks From the Pain Without Guilt

There will be moments, tiny ones at first, when you forget. When something makes you laugh, or a beautiful sunset catches your eye, or you lose yourself in a TV show, a warm bath, or a bite of your favorite food.

Then the guilt creeps in.

How can I feel joy when they're gone?

Those little breaks are not betrayals. They're medicine.

Joy does not dishonor your grief. It honors your aliveness. You're allowed to smile. You're allowed to rest. You're allowed to feel *anything*, without apologizing for it.

You are *still here*, and your ability to feel anything at all is part of what will carry you through.

Talk to Them

You loved them. Of course, you still want to talk to them.

And you get to.

Missing someone doesn't make them disappear from your heart, and talking to them doesn't make you "crazy." In fact, it makes you human. There's actually research that shows how continuing bonds—things like writing letters to your person, speaking to them out loud, or just thinking of them in daily life—can be deeply healing (Shelley, 2024). Psychologists call it a *continuing connection*. I call it what love does.

Because love like that doesn't stop just because someone is gone. It changes shape. It becomes quieter, yes, but it's still there. You still carry them. Talking to them is one way to keep that thread from snapping.

Maybe it sounds like this: "I made your banana bread today. It didn't rise properly, but it made the house smell like you, and I cried into the oven mitt."

Or this: "I saw someone with your laugh at the grocery store. I almost followed them, just to hear it again."

Or even this: "God, I need you right now. Everything's falling apart, and I wish you were here to tell me it's going to be okay."

You can whisper it into your pillow. Say it in the car. Write it down. Light a candle. Hug a sweater they used to wear and let the words spill out.

You are not talking to the past; you are talking to a love that is still very much alive inside you. And that love needs somewhere to go.

Let it go to them. Let it rise, however it wants to.

Accept That Nothing Helps and Yet Everything Matters

This part is hard to explain. In early grief, it can feel like *nothing* helps. Not the tea, not the shower, not the talking, not the crying. You do everything, and the pain is still there. Just as sharp.

But over time, something strange happens: Each small act of care leaves a trace. Each meal you eat. Each call you answer. Each breath you take. It's not that these things erase the pain; they *teach you how to carry it.*

Even when it feels like nothing is changing, these tiny acts are whispering to your nervous system: *You are safe enough to keep going.*

That's what healing starts to look like, not a sudden transformation, but a quiet return to yourself, one breath at a time.

In These Early Days, Be the Softest You Have Ever Been With Yourself

You are grieving not just a person, but a way of being, a story, a rhythm, a world that included them. That kind of rupture deserves reverence.

Don't demand strength.

Don't rush to rebuild.

Don't look for meaning just yet.

The early days are for holding yourself tenderly. For allowing the mess. For knowing that your pain is a measure of your love. And that love, *even now*, is not lost.

You are in the deep waters now. Float.

When you can't float, let yourself be held by others, memory, breath, or time.

You don't have to do this part well.

You just have to make it through. And you will.

Chapter Exercises

The "Three Things" Ritual (Daily Anchor Exercise)

When everything feels chaotic or unreal, this practice helps bring you back to the moment gently.

Each morning or evening, take a few minutes to write down:

- **One thing you did today (no matter how small):** "I brushed my teeth." / "I made tea." / "I got out of bed."
- **One thing you felt (even if it was numbness):** "I felt hollow." / "I felt angry." / "I didn't feel anything."
- **One thing that kept you here:** "The cat curled up next to me." / "A memory that came while washing dishes." / "The sound of rain."

"This Is My Grief" Statement

On a page, without needing it to be pretty or polished, finish the sentence:

"My grief feels like…"

Write as many metaphors, sensations, or images as you need.

Examples:

- *My grief feels like a heavy coat I can't take off.*
- *It feels like I'm underwater and everyone else is breathing air.*
- *It feels like fire and fog at the same time.*

Then write:

"And right now, I need…" (*Even if it's impossible, even if it's just to scream or sleep or feel nothing at all.*)

Closing Thoughts

If the early days of grief are like being caught in the undertow, pulled under by wave after wave with no sense of which way is up, then these pages have been your oxygen mask. Not to fix the pain, not to speed up the process, but simply to help you breathe long enough to see that you are still here.

You have survived something unimaginable.

You've made it through days that didn't seem survivable, days when even blinking felt like an effort. You've lived through moments when time collapsed, when the air felt too heavy, when all the colors drained from the world, and nothing tasted right. Maybe you still feel stuck in that space. That's okay. There is no expiration date on the fog.

But something subtle has already begun to shift.

Maybe you noticed a moment of quiet. A second where your body softened. A memory that made you smile through tears. A night when you finally slept. These are the fragile beginnings of something new. Not "moving on." Not forgetting. But integrating.

This is what grief does: it doesn't go away, it weaves itself into the story of who you are becoming.

In the earliest stage, the goal isn't healing. It's a shelter. It's safety. It's getting through one breath, one blink, one hour at a time. If that's all you've done, then that's everything.

But what comes next is quieter, slower, stranger: The days that start to blur into a new kind of normal. The return of routines that once felt impossible. The ache that doesn't scream anymore, but hums quietly in the background. This next part of the journey is harder to name, because it lives in the in-between.

You're no longer in the rawness of shock, but you're not "okay" either. You still miss them fiercely. You still cry without warning. However, the world has begun to ask more of you. You might even be asking more of yourself.

This is the middle stage of the grieving process. It's a lonely, complex place to be.

The check-ins have slowed. But you still carry the weight of what's missing. Now comes the deeper work: Learning how to live alongside that absence. How to carry the grief without letting it consume you. How to slowly rebuild a life that doesn't deny the loss, but makes space for it.

In the next chapter, we'll enter this strange and quiet middle. The part no one warns you about. The part where the world has moved on, but you haven't. And where, against all odds, something like life begins to return.

Chapter 7

Weathering the Middle—Living With the Absence

No one ever told me that grief felt so like fear.

— C.S. Lewis

Patricia realized she was in the middle stage of grief on a rainy Wednesday morning, the kind that used to make her text her sister just to say, "Soup weather."

She was standing in line at the grocery store, absently scrolling through her phone, when she saw a recipe for lentil stew. Without thinking, she tapped "share," ready to send it to Emily before her brain caught up with her fingers.

Her thumb hovered over her sister's name, and for the first time, she didn't cry.

There was still an ache, sharp and sudden, like pressing on a bruise, but it wasn't the kind that buckled her knees. It was quieter. Almost tender. A longing wrapped in love, not panic.

In that moment, she realized: *I've stopped expecting her to reply.*

That was the shift. Not the absence of grief, but the absence of shock.

Patricia still missed Emily with every part of her being. But she was starting to cook again. She had gone back to yoga. She'd even laughed at a joke last week—really laughed, and hadn't felt like she was betraying her sister for it.

The grief hadn't left. It never would. But it had changed shape.

That's when she knew: She was no longer in the raw, gasping beginning.

This chapter is about that stage. The strange, quiet in-between. Where the acute pain has dulled, but the longing still pulses underneath everything. Where you begin to build a new life, all while carrying the weight of the old one in your chest.

The Special Days

The birthdays still circle each year like clockwork, but now they arrive with silence instead of celebration. No phone calls. No warm hugs. No cake with laughter. Just an ache, and memories that whisper, *"She was here. She was loved."*

I light a candle to honor her, and in that soft, flickering glow, I feel her closeness again. Not as she was, but as she is now: everywhere and nowhere. Still present in a way that can't be explained, only felt.

Grief has a way of sharpening our awareness of time. The calendar becomes less about planning and more about bracing, bracing for the days that once held joy and now hold weight. These "special days" like birthdays, anniversaries, holidays,

Mother's Day, Father's Day, the day they were supposed to retire, the day they should have turned 40, carry a different kind of gravity.

They don't sneak up on you. They *loom.*

And when they arrive, they tend to pierce through whatever stability you've managed to piece together. Sometimes, the grief leading up to them is worse than the day itself. The days before an anniversary can stir something deep and restless: insomnia, irritability, and tears without cause. Your body remembers even when your mind tries not to.

And then, there are the unexpected drops. The days that aren't circled in red, but hit just as hard. Grief doesn't only wait for anniversaries; it creeps in on a random Tuesday, while folding laundry. It ambushes you in the grocery store when their favorite cereal catches your eye. It blindsides you in traffic when *that song* plays. It rises, not like a scream, but like a tide you didn't see coming.

I've learned not to fight it.

Not because it doesn't hurt, but because trying to push it down only makes it push harder. When the wave comes, I let it wash through me. I let the tears fall, the breath hitch, the memory bloom. And I remind myself, *this is love.* This ache is just love with nowhere to go. It's all the things I wish I could still give them, still share with them, still say to them.

This pain is the echo of connection. It means they mattered. It means they still do.

If you're reading this and dreading the next milestone, know this: You don't have to "celebrate" or "honor" or "mark the occasion" in any particular way. You don't have to be strong, ceremonial, or brave. You just have to get through it, whatever *that* looks like.

Light a candle. Turn off your phone. Make their favorite meal. Cancel all your plans. Cry. Laugh. Sleep. Write. Do nothing at all.

There's no right way to survive the special days. Only *your* way. That is more than enough.

Redefining Your Life Without Them

We don't always notice how much our identity is braided into the people we love. We think we're just ourselves, independent, and self-contained. But love has this way of subtly rewiring us. We pick up their phrases. We started liking the music they played around the house. We laugh a little like them. Our rhythms change because of theirs—bedtime, mealtimes, the shows we watch, and the way we spend our weekends. The life we build with them builds us in return.

So when they're gone, it's not just their absence we feel. It's the sudden lack of contour. The way we feel shapeless. It's as if someone erased a line that once defined the edge of who we were.

But slowly, gently, something else begins to happen. You start to meet a new version of yourself.

At first, this might feel strange, disloyal, even. You might think, *Who am I, if I'm not their partner? Their sibling? Their child? Their best friend?* The answer isn't simple. But it *is* sacred.

Because you are still you, and now, you are also someone shaped by loss. Someone who has loved deeply. Someone who has endured the unendurable. Someone who is still here and that matters more than you think.

This stage isn't about "starting over." That phrase can feel too clean, too final, like you're being asked to erase what came before. But you're not. You're being invited to reimagine.

To ask:

- What brings me peace now?
- What do I want to carry forward from our time together?
- What parts of me are growing because of this grief?

Redefining your life without someone you couldn't imagine living without is one of the hardest, slowest, and most sacred processes of grief. It's not about erasing the past. It's about learning to live alongside it, learning how to exist in a world that feels fundamentally changed, because it is. You are changed.

Below is a compassionate, step-by-step guide to gently discovering who you are now and who you're becoming.

Acknowledge the Gap They Left

When Marianne lost her older sister, everything in her life kept moving. The kids still needed to be fed. She was still expected to show up. The seasons changed. The mail came. But nothing *felt* real. Her sister had been her best friend, her compass. The one who made her feel seen when no one else quite could. For months, Marianne said she felt like she was missing her reflection, like she could still walk through the world, but without a center. She wasn't just mourning her sister. She was mourning the version of herself who existed *with* her.

That's what people often don't understand. Grief doesn't just take the one you love; it takes the part of *you* that existed in a relationship with them. And that's why it hurts so deeply. You're not just learning how to live without them, you're learning how to live *as someone new*.

Grief carves out space. It feels like a wound at first, raw and gaping. But eventually, slowly, and gently, that space becomes something else. A quiet room in your life that you start to furnish with meaning. A place where their voice still echoes. A place you carry with you wherever you go.

So, ask yourself:

- *What part of me feels missing without them?*
- *What parts of my life feel unrecognizable now?*
- *Where do I still carry them?*

And if the answer is: "I don't know who I am without them," then that's not weakness. That's the truth. That's the brave, terrifying, beautiful starting place of reinvention.

Because grief does not end your story, but it *does* ask you to write a new chapter.

In this chapter, you may find that the person you're becoming is stitched together with threads of who they were. That you laugh like them now, or pause the way they used to. That you say their sayings. That you love a little more fiercely. That you protect people a little more carefully.

They may be gone, but some part of them lives on in the way you live now.

Pay Attention to What Still Feels Like You

In the aftermath of loss, even the mirror can feel unfamiliar. You may not recognize your own face. But beneath the grief, small truths remain.

Start small:

- What foods bring you comfort now?
- What moments bring a flicker of peace—a cup of tea, a walk at dusk, the sound of birds?
- What activities feel soothing, or grounding, or give you a fleeting sense of *rightness*?

You're not the same person, but you're not no one either. You are *becoming*. And the things that still make you feel like *you*, even in fragments, are the clues.

Reclaim Routines or Rebuild New Ones

Daily life has a way of wrapping itself around the people we love. It's not always dramatic. It's subtle. Who cooked. Who handled the bills? The way they filled a room without trying. You don't realize how much of your routine was built around them until they're no longer there. Suddenly, the things that once felt automatic, like mornings, dinners, and weekend plans, start to feel strange. Off-balance. Empty.

That disorientation is normal. It's what happens when the structure of your life is suddenly missing a piece you always assumed would be there.

But that doesn't mean you're stuck in limbo forever. Routines don't need to be discarded; they can be rebuilt. Reimagined. Even the smallest change can offer a little bit of stability when everything else feels like it's falling apart.

Start small. Light a candle. Sit with your coffee for a few minutes without rushing. Rearrange a room, not to "move on," but to make it feel like yours again. Choose one thing each week to focus on. Not to prove you're okay, but to remind yourself you're still here.

Grief can make time feel meaningless. A day bleeds into the next. But having even one small rhythm, something you do just for yourself, can help mark the days, not as a way of forgetting, but as a way of finding your footing again. Not everything has to have meaning right now. Some things just have to get you through.

Let Yourself Want Something Again

Grief is not just sadness; it's also a silencing of desire. At first, it feels like nothing matters anymore. But eventually, a spark may return. A longing. A curiosity. A whisper that says, "I want..."

It might feel wrong to want things. It might feel like betraying your grief. But hear this clearly: Wanting again is not forgetting. Wanting is a sign that life is speaking to you again.

Let yourself want *anything*:

- to travel somewhere new
- to read a book that doesn't hurt
- to go back to school
- to laugh without guilt
- to fall in love again
- to grow a garden
- to be held

Let desire be slow, cautious, and unsure. But let it speak.

Explore Who You're Becoming

Loss changes us. That's not a flaw, it's a fact. It rearranges your inner landscape in ways you never asked for and wouldn't have chosen. But sometimes, quietly and without fanfare, it also reveals parts of you that had been waiting in the wings.

After my mom died, I didn't recognize myself for a while. I wasn't just sad; I was unmoored, hollowed out, raw in places I didn't know could ache. But somewhere in that rawness, something else started to emerge. I found that I could sit with discomfort longer than I used to. That I didn't need to run from pain, not mine, not anyone's. I became better at holding space for big feelings, even the ugly, messy ones. I became braver, not fearless, but less avoidant. More willing to stay present, even when everything in me wanted to bolt.

You might notice something similar happening to you.

You may become:

- more sensitive, more empathic.
- less tolerant of small talk and surface-level connections.
- more protective of your time, your peace, your boundaries.
- more in tune with your gut, drawn to art, solitude, ritual, or questions you never used to ask.

Let yourself be curious about this version of you. The one grief was introduced. Take long walks and ask, *Who am I now?* Journal without needing answers. Paint something without knowing why. Be alone without rushing to fill the silence.

Think of it as being more than reinvention; it's also revelation.

The loss didn't make you better, but it may have unearthed something deeper. A kind of wisdom that only comes from having loved and lost, and still choosing to keep your heart open anyway.

Carry Them Forward

Redefining your life without them doesn't mean forgetting. It doesn't mean "letting go" in the way people sometimes say it, with a tone that sounds like closing a door. It means *becoming a vessel*. A living, breathing continuation of what they meant to you.

This isn't about erasure. It's about *integration*, gathering up the threads of who they were and weaving them gently into who you are becoming.

Ask yourself:

- *What did they teach me, even without trying?*
- *What part of them still lives in how I move through the world?*
- *What phrases of theirs still echo in my head, soft and familiar as lullabies?*

Maybe your mom always made soup when someone was sick, so now you do too, instinctively. Maybe your best friend had a way of saying "Look at the moon!" every time it was full, so now you do that too, and it feels like a secret signal between worlds. Maybe your father was the kind of man who tipped too much, gave people the benefit of the doubt, or knew when silence said more than words. Now, without realizing it, you hold the door open a little longer. You say thank you a little more often. You listen a little more closely. Every time you do, *he's there.*

Carrying someone forward is not about perfect preservation. It's about *participation*. Letting their presence ripple through the choices you make, the values you uphold, and the stories you tell. Letting their love soften you, anchor you, shape you—again and again.

You don't have to "move on." You get to move *with*.

They're not just behind you. They walk beside you. In memory. In gesture. In the way you love.

This living tribute is how you keep them close without clinging. How do you turn grief into a legacy? How do you ensure that even in their absence, they remain deeply, fiercely *here*?

Give Yourself Permission to Thrive

There may come a day—unexpected, almost blasphemous—when you catch yourself laughing. Really laughing. The kind that bubbles up from somewhere deep, like spring water finding a crack in the rock.

Or you might wake one morning and feel the sun on your face and realize, with a start, that it feels *good*. You might fall in love again, or dance barefoot in your kitchen, or notice that your body is no longer clenched in defense. That your heart, though marked, is beating *boldly* again.

And with that joy may come a wave of guilt.

You might think:

- *How dare I feel this alive when they're not here to see it?*
- *Who am I to move forward when they can't?*
- *Am I betraying them by not being broken?*

But hear this, gently and clearly:

You do not owe your unending sorrow to anyone.
Not even to the ones you loved most.
Not even to the ones you would give anything to have back.
Your joy is *not* disloyalty.
It is devotion in motion.
It is proof that love doesn't end with death—it just changes forms.
And maybe the most sacred way to honor them isn't to stay in the dark.
Maybe it's to carry their light forward in you.
To become, in some small way, the very kind of miracle they would've wanted for you.
You are *still here*. And that is holy.
You are *still becoming*. And that is beautiful.
You don't have to know exactly what your new life will look like.
You just have to believe that there *is* a life on the other side of loss—
And that it can hold both your longing and your laughter, your heartbreak and your healing, your memory and your *magnificence*.
Grief does not end.
But neither does *love*.
And you, dear one, are allowed to live fully in the name of both.

Chapter Exercise

Memory Mapping

On a blank page, draw a rough outline of a heart, a tree, or even just a spiral. Inside it, write down memories of your loved one, small or big. The way they stirred their coffee. A song they loved. A time they made you laugh. When you're finished, trace over the shape again. Say their name out loud. Say: *"You are not forgotten. You're still part of my world."*

"Who Am I Now?" Self-Inventory

Loss changes us, often in ways we don't immediately recognize. Use the prompts below to gently explore who you're becoming:

- What values feel more important to me now than they did before?
- How has my view of life, death, or love changed?
- What have I learned about myself through this grief?
- What traits or strengths are surfacing that I didn't see before?

Closing Thoughts

The middle stage of grief is not as loud as the beginning, but it's no less profound. If the early stage is defined by shock and rupture, then this stage is about quiet reckoning. It's where you begin to notice that grief no longer screams; it hums. The waves still come, but you've started to learn how to float.

You've likely discovered by now that grief doesn't ask for your permission to change you, it just does. Yet, within that transformation, you also get to choose. You get to choose how to remember them. You get to choose which parts of them to carry forward. You get to choose how to meet the version of yourself who is emerging from the loss.

We've explored how to navigate this in-between space:

- How to honor their memory while still showing up for your life.
- How to sit with longing, not as a wound but as a form of enduring love.
- How to reimagine routines, reclaim your identity, and let desire return in small, flickering ways.
- How to say their name, tell their stories, and let their essence continue living in the way you live.

Grief at this stage becomes less about surviving and more about reshaping. You are not "moving on." You are moving forward with them in your heart, your habits, your voice, and your future.

As you continue this journey, the shape of your grief may soften further. It might feel less like a tidal wave and more like a quiet tide that rises and falls in the background of your days. In the next chapter, we'll talk about that stage: The later season of grief. The long-haul. The rebuilding. The places where joy returns—not because you stopped grieving, but because you've learned how to grieve and live at the same time.

Chapter 8

The Long Grief-Making Meaning Beyond the Years

In the garden of memory, in the palace of dreams... that is where we will meet again.

— Lewis Carroll

Grief doesn't end. It just changes its shape.

There comes a point—often quietly, without ceremony—when you look up and realize: You've built a new life around the absence. The dishes still need to be washed. The seasons have changed. The dog still needs walking. You may even find yourself laughing more often. Planning things. Setting goals again. Somewhere in the background of all this living, the grief is still there, but softer. Quieter. Less like a storm, more like a low tide.

Yet, every now and then, it rises.

Even in the so-called "later stages," you may find yourself caught off guard by a wave of sorrow. A memory, a scent, a familiar song, or the way someone says your name can unravel you. You might still have those crying spells. Still feel the ache of depression. Still feel the sudden, gutting absence of the person you lost. When this happens, it can be deeply confusing. *Haven't I come so far? Shouldn't I be past this by now?*

The truth is, we never "graduate" from grief. We adapt to it. We carry it differently. But it always lives in us, like a quiet room in the house of our heart.

Sometimes, when you think back to the life you had before like the way your days were structured, the small habits you shared with them, the laughter, the routines, it feels almost dreamlike. Like you're looking at a photograph of someone else's life. You know it was real. You know it shaped you. But you're no longer *in* it. You've spent so much time adjusting to this new normal that the old one starts to feel like a story you once lived in.

That's what the quote at the top of this chapter speaks to.

Lewis Carroll understood something quietly profound: When someone we love is gone, our meeting places change. We don't stop meeting them; we just meet them somewhere else. In memories. In dreams. In stories. In the strange stillness that follows a moment that reminds you of them so deeply it steals your breath.

This chapter is about *that* part of grief. The long stretch that comes after the initial chaos and numbness. When you've learned how to live without them, but you still long for them. When you've gotten used to the silence, but part of you still strains to hear their voice. It's about how to cope when the world no longer expects you to be grieving, but you still are.

Remembering Your Loved One

When someone you love dies, you don't stop loving them. You don't stop talking to them in your mind, or hearing their laugh echo in unexpected places. The bond doesn't break. It shifts. It goes underground. It becomes something invisible but no less real. Perhaps one of the greatest acts of healing we can undertake is to make the conscious choice to remember. Not in the way that anchors you to sorrow, but in a way that weaves them into the fabric of your life moving forward.

This is not about forgetting the loss. It's about keeping *life*.

The Beautiful Surprise of Memory

Grief will take many things from you, but it also gives you a strange, shimmering gift: Moments of unexpected remembering.

You'll be doing something mundane, such as folding the laundry, driving home, drinking your coffee, and suddenly, you'll remember the way they used to sing a certain song out of tune. Or how they always ate the crusts first. Or the way they'd roll their eyes when someone said something ridiculous at dinner.

You'll remember things you thought you'd forgotten. A tone of voice. A favorite phrase. A habit that used to annoy you but now feels like gold. These moments feel like the wind brushing against the curtain of your life—subtle, but unmistakably them.

Here's the miracle: Even though they are no longer physically present, you still get to know them.

Not in new moments they create, but in the memories that rise up uninvited, vivid as ever. They continue to speak through you—your gestures, your preferences, your sense of humor, your choices.

Their presence shifts from seen to felt.

Meeting Them Again, Through the World

Sometimes, you'll encounter a person who reminds you of them.

A stranger's laugh might sound *just like theirs*. Someone's handwriting might echo the notes they used to leave you. A friend might share a joke or opinion that would've made them throw their head back with laughter, and just for a second, it's like they're in the room.

Janet knows that feeling well. Her husband passed away a few years ago, but every now and then, she'll catch her son smiling at something on his phone. Not just any smile, *his* smile. That crooked, one-dimple grin he used to wear when he thought he was being clever. She'll see it flash across her son's face, and for a split second, it's like her husband is standing in the room.

That's the beautiful, surprising thing about remembering someone you've lost. You don't always have to sit down and think about them on purpose. Sometimes, they just show up in your life. In big things and in small things.

You'll be walking through your day, minding your business, and then suddenly you'll hear a song and think, *They would've loved this.* And for a moment, it's like they're with you, nodding along, smiling at your reaction.

Then there are moments when you stumble upon something like a book they would've devoured, a film they would've adored, a café they would've made "your spot," and you *know*, without a shadow of a doubt, *they would've loved this.*

A little nod from beyond. A reminder: *I'm still here. I'm still with you.*

Making Them Immortal

Regardless of your faith or even if you have none at all, I truly believe that a loved one never entirely leaves us. Their spirit lives on in the most unexpected ways: In our habits, our stories, our expressions, and the way we love others a little differently because of knowing them. As long as we remember them, speak their name, carry forward the best of what they gave us, a part of them is still here. There are countless ways to keep a loved one's memory vivid, active, and integrated into your daily life.

Tell Their Stories

One of the most powerful ways to keep someone with you is deceptively simple: Speak their name. Let them live on your tongue. Let their presence echo in your stories. Talk about them the way you'd talk about someone who just stepped out of the room.

Say things like, "My mom used to say the funniest things when she was nervous. Once she tried to talk her way out of a speeding ticket by complimenting the officer's eyebrows." Or, "My brother would've thought that was hilarious. He had the driest sense of humor, the kind that crept up on you a few seconds too late."

Janet does this all the time without even realizing it. When her son makes a face while concentrating, she smiles and says, "That's your dad's face, you know." Just like that, he's there again, in the curve of a brow, in a boy's expression, in the warm silence that follows. That's the thing about memory: When it's shared, it expands; when it's spoken aloud, it breathes.

You don't have to "let go" of someone to love them in the present tense. Every story you tell is a thread in their legacy. Every time you say their name, you are letting the world know that they mattered and still do.

Create a Ritual

It doesn't have to be elaborate. Maybe every year on their birthday, you bake their favorite cake. Or you take a walk at sunset on the day they passed. Or you light a candle and say their name aloud when you're feeling lonely.

Ritual turns remembering into reverence. It says: *You mattered, and you still do.*

Build a Memory Box or Altar

Sometimes, grief needs a place to land, something you can touch, see, and return to when the ache feels too big to carry. That's where a memory box or altar can be surprisingly comforting. It doesn't have to be elaborate. It just has to be honest.

Maybe it's a small wooden box tucked into your nightstand, filled with quiet treasures: The scarf they always wore on chilly days, a recipe card with their handwriting smudged in flour, an old photo that still makes you smile, a birthday card you've read a hundred times. Or maybe it's a tiny corner of your shelf, arranged like a whisper: Their favorite candle scent, a stone from your last walk together, a piece of jewelry they once gave you.

Whatever form it takes, this little space becomes a kind of homecoming. A place where their memory isn't abstract, it's tangible. You can sit beside it on the harder days. Talk to it. Cry. Laugh. Or simply be.

Live in a Way That Honors What They Taught You

One of the most powerful ways to keep someone's memory alive is to live in a way that honors what they taught you, not just with words, but with how you show up in the world. You become the living proof that their life mattered. That their love changed something. That they left fingerprints on your soul.

Maybe they taught you kindness, not just the polite kind but the quiet kind. The "leave extra change in the parking meter" kind. The "check in on your friend who's been distant" kind. And now, you find yourself doing those things automatically, like muscle memory. That's them, still moving through you.

Maybe they were a whirlwind of curiosity and adventure, always trying new things, starting new projects, dragging you into one harebrained scheme after another. Now, when you book a spontaneous trip or try your hand at something new, you feel them smiling somewhere in the background, like, *"That's the spirit."*

Or maybe they were the ones who taught you how to forgive. How to hold people gently. How to sit with someone else's pain without trying to fix it. And now, when you extend that same compassion to others, it's not just you doing it; it's both of you.

Living in a way that honors them doesn't mean becoming someone else. It means becoming more *yourself*, with all the pieces they helped shape. You might even surprise yourself by becoming more patient, more bold, more tender than you ever thought you could be.

Love Doesn't Die—It Transforms

When you truly love someone, they leave fingerprints on your soul. That doesn't stop when they're gone.

You may cry less over time, but you'll never stop remembering. The remembering will start to shift: From pain to presence, from ache to echo, from sorrow to something like joy.

The world may tell you that you have to "move on." But you don't. You move *with*. With the memories. With the lessons. With their voice in your head when you're facing something big. With the love they gave you, which is yours forever.

They live through you.

Through the way you speak. Through the way you care for others. Through the way you laugh, or love, or make someone else feel seen.

They live in your remembering. Every time you choose to *see them there*, to welcome them back in whatever form they show up, whether it's a breeze, a smell, a sentence, or a dream, you make them immortal again.

Because love like that doesn't die. It just changes form. And you are the living proof.

Don't Let Grief Scare You Away From Love

As the clouds begin to thin and you find yourself breathing a little easier, it's natural to start feeling protective of your newly stitched-together heart. After all, you've lived through the unthinkable. You've seen how much it hurts to lose someone you love. And now, the part of you that once loved freely might whisper: *Never again. Let's not do this again.*

This is a completely human response. When we touch fire, we recoil. When we fall, we flinch the next time we walk that same path. It makes perfect sense that part of you wants to close off, go quiet, or build a fortress around your heart. To keep yourself safe from ever having to grieve again.

But I want to gently warn you against that instinct.

Because if this book has taught you anything, I hope it's this: Grief is not a sign that something went wrong; it's a sign that something mattered.

Grief is the echo of love. It is the price of connection. It is the evidence of a life intertwined with another.

To try and live in a way that never invites grief again is to live in a way that never invites deep love, real intimacy, or meaningful vulnerability. It's a life with fewer cracks but also fewer colors.

I've seen people turn away from love after loss. I've seen them choose smaller lives, safer relationships, emotional distance, or self-sufficiency so intense it turns into isolation. They do it to protect themselves. For a while, it works, but eventually, they find that in shielding themselves from future grief, they've also shielded themselves from joy, belonging, and warmth.

You don't need to rush back into love or friendship or openness. But don't confuse your grief with a warning. It's not a reason to stop living. It's proof that you *have* lived and loved deeply.

Grief didn't break you. Grief *revealed* you. It showed you your capacity for love, your depth of feeling, your devotion, your tenderness, your strength. And that's not something to run from. That's something to honor.

So, when your heart whispers *Never again*, try answering with something softer:

- I will be careful. But I will not be closed.
- I will remember the cost. But I will still choose love.

Because this life, for all its loss and uncertainty, is still worth showing up for. Your heart—wounded, wise, and still beating, knows the way.

Chapter Exercises

Create a "Memory Garden" Journal Entry

Write a letter to the person you lost, describing how their memory shows up in your life now. Don't focus on pain, focus on presence. Where do you "meet" them these days? In what moment did you last feel close to them?

You can use this prompt to start: *"Today I remembered you when..."*

Repeat this any time grief rises unexpectedly. It helps anchor you in the ongoing bond.

Notice When You're Closing Off

Over the next week, gently observe your reactions to connection:

- Do you recoil from intimacy, affection, or emotional openness?
- Do you avoid situations that might bring joy *because* they might also bring loss?

Each time you notice it, don't judge it. Just write, *"I felt myself closing off when... but I stayed open by..."*

Even a small act like saying yes to coffee or smiling back is a win. Track it.

The "Still With Me" List

List five ways your loved one still lives on in you today. Think beyond just habits, consider how they've shaped your worldview, your kindness, your boundaries, your quirks. For each, write:

- The trait or action.
- A small moment when you recently expressed it.
- How does that make you feel?

This helps you recognize that *you carry them*, not just in memory, but in motion.

Closing Thoughts

Grief is not a straight road, and it's certainly not a checklist. There is no finish line, no final "stage" where you earn a gold star and never feel the ache again. What there *is*, however, is a quiet transformation. A re-weaving. A gentle, gradual process by which the raw, tearing absence becomes something softer, something that no longer stops your world, but lives inside it.

This chapter has explored that subtle evolution: How love continues in new forms, how memory can surprise us with comfort, how grief can coexist with laughter, forward movement, and even joy. You've learned that remembrance doesn't have to weigh you down; it can carry you. That rituals, stories, and small everyday moments can become sacred meeting places. Most importantly, the pain of grief is not a sign to stop loving, but proof that you already have.

We've talked about keeping your heart open, not in spite of the pain, but *because* of it. Because you now know how deep love can go. Because you've lived through the loss and come out wiser, more attuned, and infinitely more human.

But what if none of this is your experience?

What if you're not feeling lighter yet? What if your grief has refused to soften? What if your timeline looks nothing like what this chapter describes?

You're not alone.

In the next chapter, we'll talk about what happens when grief *doesn't* follow a neat path. When it lingers in unexpected ways. When it flares up months or years later. We'll explore complicated grief and what to do when grief happens alongside existing mental health struggles. Because not every healing journey fits the map. That's okay.

Grief isn't a process to complete. It's a relationship you learn how to live with. Let's keep walking, wherever you are on the path.

Chapter 9

Grief That Lingers, and What to Do About It

> *I sat with my anger long enough, until she told me her real name was grief.*
>
> — C.S. Lewis (paraphrased)

I n the last three chapters, we spoke of grief as though it moves through distinct seasons: The early days of shock and unraveling, the blurry middle where life begins to reassemble itself around the absence, and the quiet stretch of moving forward while still carrying what was lost. Sometimes, maybe even often, grief *does* move in a way that roughly follows that rhythm. Not cleanly. Not on schedule. But gradually, with softness and setbacks, many people find themselves inching towards peace.

But sometimes, that peace never comes.

Grief doesn't always follow a roadmap, and love doesn't always loosen its grip just because time has passed. I had a friend who lost his teenage daughter in the late 2000s. She was bright and fierce, with a sarcastic laugh and a heart that beat like a drum for justice. One minute, he was helping her fill out college applications. Next, he was picking out her headstone.

In the beginning, he did what people are supposed to do. He took time off work. He went to therapy once or twice. He attended the funeral, thanked the people who brought food, and even wrote a eulogy he barely remembers reading.

And then life went on. But he didn't.

He stayed frozen in the wreckage while the world rebuilt itself around him. For years, he couldn't walk past a school without nausea. He kept her bedroom exactly as she left it, not in a loving, shrine-like way, but like a room he didn't dare enter because he was afraid of what the silence would do to him. He avoided birthdays. He skipped holidays. He stopped answering friends' calls, and every year, on the anniversary of her death, he'd sit in his car, parked outside the cemetery, unable to go in.

"I should be getting better," he told me once, nearly a decade later. "But I still feel like it happened yesterday."

That's when he realized something wasn't right.

This wasn't just grief; it was grief that had become stuck.

Complicated grief (also known now as Prolonged Grief Disorder) is what happens when the pain of loss doesn't soften with time. It doesn't ease. It hardens. It calcifies into your daily life. It keeps you looping through guilt, isolation, or numbness, long after the world assumes you've "moved on." For him, it looked like this:

- Avoiding reminders of her photos, stories, even her name.
- A deep, unshakeable belief that he could've saved her.
- Anger that burned low but was constant.

It took him 10 years to say out loud what he'd feared the most: *"I'm still not okay."*

This chapter is for those moments.

When the fog doesn't lift. When the anniversaries don't get easier. When your heart still screams in a world that has gone quiet.

If that's where you are, whether it's been one year or ten, I want you to know this: You are not broken. Your grief is not wrong. But you *may need help finding your way back.*

What Is Complicated Grief?

Let's start with a truth that's tender and often terrifying to admit: Some grief doesn't soften with time.

Some grief roots itself so deeply that even years later, it still feels like the world ended yesterday. It's not just sadness that comes and goes. It's a kind of emotional paralysis. It doesn't move through you, it moves *into* you, sets up camp, and makes itself at home in your chest.

This is what mental health professionals sometimes call Complicated Grief, or more recently, Prolonged Grief Disorder (PGD). It's when grief doesn't follow the arc we're often told it "should." It doesn't ease or settle. It doesn't gently integrate into the rhythm of your days. Instead, it stays raw. Loud. Unbearable.

Here's the most important thing I can say about it: This is not a failure. This is not weakness. This is not a sign that you're grieving "wrong." It's a wound that never had the space, support, or safety it needed to begin to heal.

"Normal" grief, if we can even use that word, is like a tide. It washes over you in waves. Some days, you can stand in it. Some days it knocks you down. But slowly, over time, the waves become a little more manageable. They still hit hard sometimes, but they don't pull you under the way they once did.

Complicated grief is different. It doesn't ebb. It loops. It's persistent, unyielding, and often invisible to the outside world. While others expect you to "be better by now," you're still waking up every day to a kind of heartbreak that feels just as fresh, if not worse, than when it first began.

You might be experiencing complicated grief if:

- It's been over a year, and the sorrow still feels *all-consuming*.
- You find it hard to accept the loss, even intellectually.
- You go out of your way to avoid reminders of the person, even things you used to treasure.
- You feel like life has lost its meaning or color.
- You have trouble functioning at work, in relationships, or in daily life.
- You feel stuck in a loop of "if only" and "what if," unable to move forward or even sideways.
- You may even feel angry at the person for dying, and then ashamed for feeling that way.

If this sounds familiar, I want you to hear me clearly: This isn't just sadness. It's a kind of trauma.

It means the loss was so seismic—so profoundly disruptive to your inner world—that your mind and body haven't yet found a way to make sense of it. You're not weak. You're not broken. You're in pain.

Pain, especially pain this deep, needs more than time. It needs tenderness. It needs acknowledgment. Sometimes, it needs help from someone trained to hold space for the complexity you're carrying.

You do not have to grieve alone. You are allowed to ask for help. Healing, even now, is still possible.

When Grief Intersects With Mental Health

If you were already living with anxiety, depression, PTSD, bipolar disorder, OCD, or any other mental health condition, grief can push those symptoms into overdrive. It can undo the balance you've worked hard to build. Or, it might pull forward something you hadn't noticed before, something that was quiet until the loss cracked everything open.

Even if you've never had a diagnosis, the emotional intensity of grief can look and feel a lot like mental illness. That's where things get complicated, and often misunderstood, even by ourselves.

You might wonder:

- *Is this depression or just grief?*
- *Is this anxiety or just fear of another loss?*
- *Is this PTSD or just memory?*
- *Am I falling apart, or is this just what grief does?*

The truth is: Sometimes it's both.

Loss destabilizes us. That destabilization can awaken mental health challenges that were dormant, deepen ones we already manage, or even mask them in a cloud of grief so dense we can't tell where one ends and the other begins.

Grief and Depression

Lisa lost her brother six months ago. In the first few weeks, she cried constantly. She couldn't sleep, she forgot to eat, she kept picking up her phone to text him before remembering. Her friends checked in, and she talked about him often. She still laughed at memories, even through tears. That was grief in its natural, raw form—loud, disorienting, but still alive.

But now, something has shifted.

Lisa no longer cries. In fact, she doesn't feel much of anything. Her friends stopped calling because she stopped replying. Her brother's once comforting photos now just feel like static. She can't remember the last time she showered. Food tastes like cardboard. She scrolls endlessly through her phone, not even reading. Her thoughts have started to circle a quiet, scary place: *"What's the point?"* Not "I want to die," but... *"I'm not really living."*

How Do You Know the Difference?

Grief and depression can look like twins at first glance—fatigue, tearfulness, disinterest in life. But if you sit with them long enough, you'll start to feel their different pulses.

Grief	Depression
Comes in waves.	Feels like a flatline.
Triggered by memories, anniversaries, and reminders.	Feels constant and unrelenting.
Still allows moments of laughter, love, and connection.	Feels like nothing breaks through.
Pain is about the *loss*.	Pain is about *you*—feeling worthless, empty, broken.
Longing to connect with the person who's gone.	Desire to disconnect from *everything*.
You miss them.	You forget how to miss anyone, including yourself.

The Most Telling Sign?

When you're grieving, you may feel devastated, but there's still a *thread of meaning*. You might say, "I wish they were here" or "I don't know how I'll live without them," but there's still a *desire* to live.

With depression, the desire starts to dim. You might not *want* to die, but you also don't want to be alive. It feels like life is something happening to someone else, and you're just floating through it in grayscale.

What To Do If This Is You

Firstly, *you are not broken*. This doesn't mean you've failed at grieving. It means your pain has deepened into a place that needs more light, more support, more holding, and you don't have to carry that alone.

- **Talk to someone.** A therapist, a support group, a compassionate friend. You don't need to "explain" your grief perfectly. You just need to be witnessed.
- **Reintroduce gentle structure.** A daily walk. Drinking water. Brushing your teeth. Tiny things. They are not small when everything feels heavy.
- **Ask your doctor for help.** Sometimes grief opens a door to clinical depression. There is no shame in this. Medication and therapy can be life-saving tools, not signs of weakness.
- **Look for moments of beauty.** Not to distract yourself, but to remind your body that life still holds color, even when your heart can't feel it yet.

You loved them. And now you're hurting. That's not a pathology. That's proof of your capacity for love.

But if the hurting becomes too quiet, too numb, and too dark, let someone in. Let someone turn on a light.

Grief asks to be witnessed. Depression asks to be answered.

You deserve both.

Grief and Anxiety

Grief doesn't always weep quietly. Sometimes, it paces. Sometimes, it trembles. Sometimes, it clutches your chest and won't let go.

After a loss, anxiety can become your unwelcome shadow. It might show up in the middle of the night, a flutter in your ribs like something's wrong, even when nothing is. You might check your phone compulsively, dreading bad news. You might find yourself fearing everything: phone calls, hospital smells, sirens, silence.

A friend of mine, Leo, lost his father suddenly to a heart attack. But if you ask him when the grief began, he doesn't say the day his father died. He says it started months earlier, after his dad collapsed once at work and the doctors began using words like *risk, weakening,* and *if it happens again.*

Leo described those weeks like being stuck in a slow-motion car crash: "You're not hit yet, but you know you're going to be, and the dread is constant. I couldn't sleep. I was always waiting for something. My body didn't trust the future."

That's anticipatory grief.

It's what happens when the loss hasn't happened yet, but your heart begins to mourn anyway. It's often seen when someone you love is terminally ill, but it can also begin the moment you hear news of an accident, a diagnosis, or any shift that whispers: *I might lose them.*

It's not imaginary. It's not selfish. It's real grief. And it lives in your chest, in your breath, in your rituals. You might cry while making coffee, imagining mornings without them. You might picture their empty chair at dinner, even while they're still alive. You might start to pull away emotionally, not because you don't love them, but because you do, and it hurts too much to stay soft.

Anticipatory grief is confusing because it can make you feel disloyal or dramatic, like you're grieving too soon. But this, too, is love, just wearing its armor. Your mind is trying to protect you from devastation. Your body is rehearsing loss in the hope that it might hurt less when it finally comes.

Even after death, the anxiety doesn't always go away. Grief and anxiety tangle together like roots. You begin to fear more loss. You wake up expecting disaster. You might avoid joy because joy now feels fragile. You might try to control everything around you because you couldn't control *that*.

If this is where you are: pause. Breathe. Place a hand on your heart.

You're not broken. You are grieving.

Your nervous system is trying to shield you from a world that suddenly feels unsafe. But safety *can* return. You will not feel this vigilant forever. The alarms will be quiet. The breath will slow. Joy will become less terrifying.

But for now, it's okay to hold your fear gently, instead of fighting it.

You've been through the unthinkable. Of course, your heart is still bracing for impact.

Grief and PTSD

Some losses don't just break your heart, they fracture your sense of safety, of time, of reality itself.

When a death is sudden, violent, or deeply distressing, like a car crash, a suicide, a brutal accident, or a hospital call that came too late, it doesn't just create grief. It creates *shock*. And sometimes, that shock doesn't go away.

This is where grief begins to overlap with post-traumatic stress.

You may find yourself stuck in the moment it happened, reliving it over and over. The ring of the phone in the middle of the night. The sterile chill of the hospital corridor. The silence that followed someone saying, "We did everything we could."

These memories don't fade with time. They *intrude*. Flashbacks come like a punch to the chest. You hear a siren and your body tenses. You see a photo, and suddenly you're right back in the moment when the world split open. You might flinch at the sound of their name, avoid familiar places, or refuse to talk about what happened—not because you don't care, but because your nervous system is on overdrive, trying to protect you from shattering.

Let me tell you about Mia.

Mia lost her younger brother in a motorcycle accident. One moment, she was folding laundry. Next, her phone rang, and everything blurred. She remembers screaming, collapsing in the hallway, and the feel of the tiles against her cheek.

Weeks later, Mia couldn't drive past the intersection where the crash happened. She avoided highways completely. Loud engines made her nauseous. She wasn't just sad, she was *stuck*. She kept dreaming she was trying to save him, arriving too late. She couldn't focus at work. She stopped returning calls. Her world shrank to the size of her fear.

It took her months to realize what she was experiencing wasn't "just grief," it was trauma. And that difference mattered. Because it meant she wasn't crazy. She wasn't weak. Her mind and body were simply reacting to the unthinkable.

If any of this sounds familiar, know this: you're not alone. And you're not overreacting.

Grief is the ache of love with nowhere to go. Trauma is the wound that never got a chance to close.

You may need help grieving *the person* but also help revisiting *the moment* safely, with someone trained to guide you through it without pulling you under again.

Because what happened *to you* matters too.

This is not just about moving forward. It's about making peace with the memory that keeps chasing you and finding solid ground again.

Making the First Step

If you're reading this and thinking, *"Maybe I need help,"* start there. That thought alone is your first signpost. And the good news? You don't have to figure everything out today. You just have to begin.

Here's how.

Start by naming it out loud, if you can. Say something simple, clear, and true:

- I think I need someone to talk to.
- I've been stuck for a while.
- This isn't getting better, and I don't know what to do.

You don't need to have the perfect words. The goal is to interrupt the spiral of silent suffering. Once you name it, you can begin to take action.

Step 1: Talk to Your Doctor

Your primary care physician can be a helpful first stop. Tell them what's been going on—sleeplessness, irritability, numbness, panic, whatever it is. They can refer you to a grief counselor, psychologist, or support group. If it feels too awkward to say it out loud, write it down and hand it over.

Step 2: Search Locally

Use trusted directories like Psychology Today, TherapyRoute.com (international), or ask your local hospice or hospital for referrals. Search for:

- Grief therapist near me.
- Bereavement counselor + your city.
- Trauma-informed therapist + grief.

Look for someone with experience in grief and loss. If complicated grief or trauma is in the mix, aim for someone trained in prolonged grief disorder (PGD) or trauma therapy (like EMDR or somatic therapy).

Step 3: Ask a Trusted Friend to Help

If you're too overwhelmed to make calls or browse websites, ask someone you trust to help you search, schedule, or even accompany you to your first appointment. It doesn't make you needy, it makes you human.

Step 4: Try a Support Group

Grief groups, online or in person, can be life-changing. Look for groups through local churches, hospitals, community centers, or platforms like GriefShare, Reddit's r/GriefSupport, or The Dinner Party (for young adults who've lost someone close). Sometimes, just hearing "me too" changes everything.

Step 5: Keep It Low-Pressure

The first counselor might not be the right fit. That's okay. You're allowed to try again. Think of it like dating; it's not failure, it's refinement. Don't quit because one person didn't understand. Keep looking until someone does.

Step 6: Take the First Action Today

Not tomorrow. Not "when things calm down." Today. Search for one name. Write one email. Send one text. That's movement. That's momentum.

You don't need a five-step plan or a roadmap to healing. You just need a place to start. And often, that place is as simple as asking: "Who can help me carry this?"

Start there.

Chapter Exercises

Track the Terrain of Your Grief

Over the next week, spend five minutes a day journaling about how your grief feels *in that moment*. Don't worry about eloquence—just name it:

- Does it feel heavy or hollow?
- Are you avoiding something today?
- Did something trigger a wave?

At the end of the week, look back and circle any patterns. Awareness is the first step toward change.

Map Your Support System

On a blank page, draw three circles:

- **Inner circle:** People you can be raw and real with.
- **Middle circle:** Those you trust but keep things lighter with.
- **Outer circle:** Resources, support groups, professionals, books, online spaces.

Notice any gaps? Is there someone you want to bring closer? Is there a name you've been too scared to write down but might need to?

Closing Thoughts

Over the course of this book, we've walked through the many faces of grief. We've talked about the shock of early loss, the messiness of the middle, and the slow, uneven return to a life that will never be the same, but can still be full. We've explored memory, identity, and the aching paradox of healing: That it doesn't mean forgetting, and it doesn't mean moving on. It means moving *with*.

And in this final chapter, we sat with the heaviest truth of all: Sometimes grief gets stuck. Sometimes time doesn't soften it—because the wound was too deep, the love too fierce, or the loss too entangled with trauma, mental health, or isolation. We named this complicated grief not to diagnose or label, but to shine a light on what so often hides in the shadows. We said, out loud, what so many are afraid to admit: *I'm still not okay.*

If that's where you are, I hope this chapter met you there with honesty, with care, and with a reminder that you are not broken. You are not too late. And you do not have to carry this alone.

If you're further along and reading this with the bittersweet distance of time passed, I hope it helped you better understand yourself or someone you love.

This is the last chapter in the book, but it isn't the last chapter in *your* story.

There is no final page in grief. No clean ending. No perfect closure. What there is, instead, is *continuation*—a life after the loss, shaped by it, strengthened by it, and still open to beauty.

Whether your grief feels loud or quiet today, whether you're still in the thick of it or just learning to live with the scar, I want to thank you. For reading. For feeling. For staying with yourself through the storm.

You may not have chosen this loss. But you are choosing every day to keep living.

That matters. *You* matter.

May this book be not just a companion for your pain, but a witness to your courage. You have come so far. Whatever comes next, you will not face it alone.

Conclusion

Grief is not something you conquer. It is not a battle you win or a mountain you summit. It's something you learn to walk alongside—sometimes limping, sometimes crawling, and sometimes standing still with your hands on your knees, trying to catch your breath. Yet, through every stage of this difficult, sacred journey, you have done the bravest thing of all: you have stayed. You've stayed with your heart, with your pain, with the memory of what was. You've given yourself the most important gift there is, the permission to feel, to fall apart, to rebuild, and to love again, even inside the ache.

Throughout these pages, we've explored what it means to meet grief at the door, to let it in rather than shut it out. We've named the numbness, the shock, the guilt, the yearning, and the loneliness. We've spoken to the silence that settles in after the funeral, to the waves that crash out of nowhere at the grocery store, to the haunting disorientation of waking up in a world that's missing someone you never imagined living without. But we've also explored what it means to keep going, not despite the pain, but with it. Not by pretending to be strong, but by learning to be soft in a world that often demands you harden.

Healing, we've learned, is not about forgetting or moving on. It's about weaving the love you still carry into the life you're learning to live now. It's about honoring the bond without being crushed by the absence and about discovering that your heart is bigger than you thought, not because it stopped hurting, but because it learned to stretch around the hurt. You've discovered ways to breathe through the unbearable—tools like journaling, grounding rituals, quiet self-compassion, and mindful reflection. None of them is magic. None of them cures. But each one has a small, steady hand on your back, reminding you that you are not lost, just altered.

Now, as you close this book, I hope you don't feel that something has ended, but that something new has opened. This isn't the conclusion of your grief story. It's a gentle turning of the page. What you do with the tools you've gathered is up to you now. There's no right way to grieve, no perfect rhythm to follow. Just small, sacred steps forward. Let yourself move slowly. Let yourself celebrate memories without guilt. Let yourself feel joy again, even as you carry the weight of what was lost. Make room for both. There is space for it all.

Grief may have changed you, but it has not emptied you. In many ways, it has made you more tender, more honest, more open to the fragile beauty of being alive. The brokenness you feared would define you may have instead revealed your truest self. And though you may always walk with a limp, that limp tells the story of someone who has loved deeply, lived fully, and dared to keep going with a heart that remembers.

So, as you move forward, on your terms, in your time, carry this with you: Healing is not linear, and that's not a flaw. Love never dies, it only changes form. Your story is still unfolding, and there is more to write.

Thank you for allowing me to walk beside you in this part of your story. May you find peace in unexpected places, strength in quiet moments, and love in every breath, every memory, and in every step.

You are not alone.

Dear Heart

I see you.
You—who wake up each day with a quiet ache no one else can hear.
You—who carry the weight of loss in your chest while the world rushes on, as if nothing has changed.
You—who smile for others, but cry alone in the stillness, wondering if anyone truly understands.
This letter is for you—the silent griever, the brave soul walking through invisible pain.
I want you to know: your grief is valid. It counts. Even if you don't have words for it.
Even if no one's asked *"How are you?"* in a long time.
Even if it's been months... or years... and people expect you to be "better by now."
There is no right way to grieve.
No schedule. No finish line. No blueprint to follow.
Grief doesn't obey timetables—it moves in spirals, in waves, in quiet cycles.
You are not doing it wrong. You are not broken.
You are healing—slowly, deeply, and in your own sacred way.
So, if all you did today was breathe, that is enough.
If you miss them more today than yesterday—that's okay.

If you still talk to them, still cry for them, still laugh at their memory—that's love. That's connection. That's what it means to be human.

Let the silence cradle your grief like a soft, warm blanket.
Let your heart, break open—not with shame, but with grace.
Let your pain remind you: you loved deeply. You still do.
You don't have to grieve loudly to be heard.
You don't have to explain your sorrow to be understood.
And you don't have to be strong every day.
You are enough—exactly as you are.
With love,
Your Fellow Traveler in Grief

Thank You Note

Dear Reader,

Thank you for welcoming me into your hearts, for choosing this book as your companion, and for allowing its words to walk alongside you.

Congratulations on taking the first step and doing it on your terms; it is truly something to acknowledge. I'm grateful you made space for this message and allowed me to be part of your journey.

Leaving a review is a simple way to support independent authors, like me. Your feedback would mean a great deal, as it helps me continue writing books that offer comfort, encouragement, and healing support.

To leave a review, please visit: https://mybook.to/MeetingGrief

Thank you again,

Nicole De Coteau

References

- Alighieri, D. (2010). *The Divine comedy*. Penguin Books. (Original work published 1321)
- Brown, B. (2013, January 15). Shame vs. guilt. *Brené Brown*. https://brenebrown.com/articles/2013/01/15/shame-v-guilt/
- Jones, L. (2025). Grief quotes to comfort and carry you through loss. *21 Ninety*. https://21ninety.com/grief-quotes
- Kübler-Ross, E. (2005). *On grief and grieving*. Scribner's.
- Lewis, C. S. (n.d.). A quote by C.S. Lewis. *Goodreads*. https://www.goodreads.com/quotes/10559483-i-sat-with-my-anger-long-enough-until-she-told
- Mayo Clinic Staff. (2017, May 16). Depersonalization-derealization disorder. *Mayo Clinic*. https://www.mayoclinic.org/diseases-conditions/depersonalization-derealization-disorder/symptoms-causes/syc-20352911
- Rebecca. (2024, February 14). 40 quotes that will inspire you to be gentle with yourself. *Minimalism Made Simple*. https://www.minimalismmadesimple.com/home/be-gentle-with-yourself-quotes/
- Shelley. (2024, March 7). *Continuing bonds theory in grief counselling*. The Loss Foundation. https://thelossfoundation.org/continuing-bonds-theory-in-grief-counselling/
- Smith, C. B. (2025, March 19). This is your brain on grief. *Oprah Daily*. https://www.oprahdaily.com/life/health/a64232900/how-grief-rewires-the-brain/
- Tyrrell, P., Harberger, S., Schoo, C., & Siddiqui, W. (2023). Kübler-Ross stages of dying and subsequent models of grief. *StatPearls*. National Library of Medicine. https://www.ncbi.nlm.nih.gov/books/NBK507885/
- Unknown. (2015). A quote by Unknown. *Tiny Buddha*. https://tinybuddha.com/wisdom-quotes/be-gentle-with-yourself-youre-doing-the-best-you-can/
- Wu, P. F., & Bernardi, R. (2020). Community attachment and emotional well-being: An empirical study of an online community for people with diabetes. *Information Technology & People, ahead-of-print*(ahead-of-print). https://doi.org/10.1108/itp-06-2019-0293

- Zunin, H. S. (2025). A quote by Hilary Stanton Zunin. *Goodreads*. https://www.goodreads.com/author/quotes/688159.Hilary_Stanton_Zunin

Printed in Dunstable, United Kingdom